MW00874531

The Leadership Code

Jan,

You are one of the strongest
& best leaders I know.

Enjoy!

Love from
Wanda

2017

The Leadership Code

*People-Focused, Values-Based Leadership
for Maximum Performance*

AJ Slivinski

ISBN-13: 978-1505397703

Dedication

For my "Bare."
I would not be who I am today without your ongoing love and support over the last 34 years together.

Contents

Acknowledgements

This book is about leadership. To a very great extent, leadership is learned through the example and coaching of others and this was certainly true in my case. Throughout my life and career there have been so many who have contributed to my development as a leader.

Many individuals in the groups I've listed below imparted to me the values by which I've led and live today. I am extremely grateful to the many people represented in these groups and owe them a great debt.

My early career revolved around Maple Leaf Foods in Canada. My bosses at Maple Leaf Foods saw potential in me, supported me, and became my mentors. My peers and employees worked hard for me, trusted me, and contributed significantly to our great success. Many of these people are still my good friends today.

Later in my career, I enjoyed launching a Contact Center in Cyprus for Cryptologic/WagerLogic. The team and camaraderie that we developed there was incredible. As a team we tested and honed the ideas communicated in this book. Armed with those ideas we accomplished world-class performance together. Our success as a team and the processes we used to get there form the premise of this book.

I also wish to acknowledge all the "A" people in my life—both at work and in my personal life. You all know who you are and I'm very grateful to you. You continually exceeded my expectations in every area of my life. Your example has challenged me and serves as the standard by which I evaluate all others. You are undeniably instrumental in my success and I thank you all.

As you'll see, my family has had a profound impact on my life and success as a leader as well. My parents, grandparents, sister, aunts and uncles taught me foundational values like: respect, drive, discipline, dedication, honesty and empathy. I would not be who I am today without their love, support and guidance.

I appreciate Rob Fischer for his work ghostwriting and editing my book. He patiently took the time to pore over all my notes and listen to my story. His background in leadership development and as a writer made him the perfect choice for gathering and clarifying my thoughts.

I am also grateful to Ray Edwards for his spiritual guidance, encouragement and facilitation in the process of writing this book.

— *AJ Slivinski*

Foreword

This is an era of unprecedented difficulty and opportunity in business. The difficulty does not require elaboration from me; you are undoubtedly already familiar with it.

What of the opportunity? The fundamental principles of good and profitable business are just as valid as ever. They still work to produce companies and products that both create profits and change the world for the better.

The challenge is how to separate the difficulty from the opportunity, and then how to have the integrity to aspire to meet both of the inherent potentials of the opportunity: to create maximum profits while doing maximum good. These two are not mutually exclusive, but represent an intersect point on a graph. You will always find this point "up and to the right."

Where do we find guidance on this quest for the ideal business – the one that profits the stakeholders and also changes the world for the better? How do we employ principles that profit the company stakeholders and employees, as well as make life better for the customers of that company?

A good place to start is the book you are now reading. In The Leadership Code, AJ Slivinski shares the insights of decades of successful corporate leadership. His fundamental revelation is: leaders do not lead companies, they lead people.

The Leadership Code unveils his proven, time-tested philosophy of the three essential themes required to successfully take the helm of any organization: leadership, people, and values.

Any of these three by itself, without the others, will not bring the ultimate success you desire. You need a solid, practical, and actionable plan to blend these three important factors into the recipe for ultimate success: a profitable business that serves stakeholders, employees, and customers alike.

I urge you to not only read this book, but to put the principles into practice.

You have the guidance you need in your hands. What you will do with it is up to you.

—Ray Edwards
Redding, CA 2014

Introduction

If you've ever traveled in Europe, you've no doubt enjoyed their delicious, old-world breads. These breads are so substantial and satisfying it's no wonder many Europeans take two bread meals per day. Breaking open and savoring a fresh-baked loaf is one of life's simple pleasures!

What has puzzled me over the years, however, is why we can't seem to reproduce those hard-crusted, full-bodied breads back in Canada or the US. It seems that a baker can mix the same ingredients here, yet the finished product doesn't taste, look, or feel anything like its European counterpart.

As a business executive and entrepreneur for more than 25 years, I've found that leadership has much in common with bread-making. Two leaders can seemingly take the same "ingredients" and apply them to their businesses: one will succeed and the other will fail. Obviously, a leader must begin with the right "ingredients" or failure is certain.

The truth is that leaders are far more accustomed to failing than succeeding at business. Consider US business startups, for instance: 25 percent fail in their first year; 55 percent after five years; and 71 percent after 10 years.[1]

Perhaps you ask, "Yes, but what about the Fortune 500 companies? Surely they fare better than that!" Business Week reports, "The average life expectancy of a multinational corporation—Fortune 500 or its equivalent—is between 40 and 50 years."[2]

At the inception of Forbes in 1917, they developed *The Forbes Top 100* performing companies roster. Of those top 100 companies, only one—General Electric is still on the list.[3]

Harvard School of Business presses the point even further when it suggests that if we were to define business failure in terms of failing to realize projected return on investment, then business failure rate stands at 70 to 80 percent. If we tighten the definition of failure even further so that if a company makes a financial projection, but falls short in meeting it, then 90 to 95 percent of businesses fail.[4]

Could it be that the success of a baker or a leader is not merely in the ingredients they use but how they blend those ingredients? Over my years in management, I've watched (and sometimes participated in) organizations that seemed to have the right "ingredients," yet they made the same mistakes over and over again resulting in failure.

On the other hand, I've had the privilege of learning from others whose businesses have thrived. I've also applied what I learned from them and have watched my own businesses grow and excel. The result of all of this was that in just three years, we were able to take a two-person organization to 120 employees serving customers in 12 languages. We had to recruit 70 percent of those employees from outside the country. Yet, within those few short years we were recognized and awarded as the number one contact center in the world.

Let me whet your appetite for where this book will take you and your business. What I'm about to share with you is not mere theory, but highly practical. Nor is this information new—but we tend to forget—so I've repackaged it in a way to get your attention and that will assist in The Leadership Code implementation.

The core message of this book centers around three essential themes: *leadership, people* and *values*. Consider the following in terms of these three themes.

LEADERSHIP

- ⁂ Many CEOs and managers attempt to lead a *business* instead of leading *people*. This is a fundamental flaw of business leadership.
- ⁂ Effective leaders lead from *values* and provide a clear *vision* and *mission* for the organization.
- ⁂ A leader must build trust, over-communicate and measure everything.
- ⁂ In terms of leadership style, most leaders tend toward one of two extremes: either direct or consensus leadership. Defaulting to either extreme will prove his/her undoing.

PEOPLE

- ⁂ A business without its people is merely an inanimate machine.
- ⁂ Organizations that focus first on people have the best results. (GE is testimony to this.)
- ⁂ Companies with high levels of employee engagement are more productive, perform better financially, and boast higher customer and employee retention rates.

※ We must hire and promote based on values (character) *and* skills and performance.

VALUES

※ Values define the identity and character of the company.

※ Core values provide the guiding principles upon which a company is founded and on which it operates on a daily basis.

※ Values must be at the center of all decision-making in an organization.

※ Core values are the primary recruiting, evaluating and retention tools of an organization.

※ The CEO and all management staff must live and lead by these values at all times.

This people-centric, values-focused theme represents the core message of this book. I'm excited to share with you our experiences and stories related to this core message. As I'm sure you will see it's not just about having the right ingredients but more importantly the manner in which you blend them that ensures success.

—*AJ Slivinski*

CHAPTER ONE

Fail Point

People buy into the leader before they buy into the vision.
– John C. Maxwell

JIM'S STORY

Jim's dad started his business many years ago out of his garage. His dad had always liked to tinker and make things that people wanted. He capitalized on his skills and built a business around them.

The business continued to grow, so he transitioned out of his garage into his own shop, and then eventually to a large-scale operation. The growth of his business was quite impressive and they continued to hire more and more people.

Everyone from his employees to his customers liked Jim's dad. He was thought of very highly and became a leader in the community. Many of his closest friends were among his customers.

Jim joined the business in his 20s and began working alongside of his dad. But everyone associated the business with his dad—Jim was merely his son. Jim's dad continued running the business and functioned as the "face" of the business.

After some years, Jim's dad became ill and retired. Not long afterward he died. While Jim continued to run the business, ownership of the business had been distributed to Jim *and* his siblings. As is often the case, Jim could not seem to live up to the expectations of his siblings when it came to running the business.

What made matters worse is that the business began to decline. Sales eroded, overheads rose, and profits sank. Jim knew something must be missing, but for the life of him, he couldn't figure out what. Most of his employees had worked for his dad, so the tribal knowledge and the same players were still there.

In desperation, Jim tried everything: he attended conferences, read books, watched DVDs, attended training, and he hired consultants. The consultants seemed to offer cookie-cutter solutions that never stuck. The binders they left behind only collected dust on bookshelves. Their commitment to his company was shallow. He felt used by them.

In moments of reverie after a motivating conference, Jim dreamed of restoring the business to its former glory and even surpassing what his father had built. If only he could figure out what his father had done differently to be so successful!

But back at the business, Jim was up to his eyeballs in paperwork and putting out fires with disgruntled customers. He had delegated all people issues to HR. He was never comfortable dealing with the people issues anyway and had never been trained to do so.

The business was falling through his fingers like sand. He became desperate for a different kind of solution, perhaps a new kind of consultant or some secret business formula.

Occasionally, Jim had moments of clarity. He saw that the business needed a clear vision and strategic plan. A lofty goal around which he could rally his people seemed paramount.

Yes, his *people*—the *employees*. Perhaps if he could muster their expertise...but did he have the right people? How could he know whether he had the right people? He tossed that notion aside as something beyond his reach. He didn't have the time or knowhow to take on that beast. There were just too many other demands.

As the business continued to decline, morale began to deteriorate. Back-talk among managers became common and cliques formed within departments. Jim's best performers began leaving and joining the competition, which worsened matters considerably.

Jim felt the ever-growing weight of what was happening to his business. His family didn't understand what Jim was experiencing and he felt uncomfortable talking to them about it. As a result, his relationships with his family and siblings deteriorated. He felt like he had no one to talk to.

Jim's health began to suffer and he began to withdraw socially until he eventually became depressed. His life and his business seemed out of control.

Soon, Jim despised going to work and looked for ways to avoid his responsibilities. He felt the only way out of this pit was to sell the business. But who would buy a business in decline? He knew he would never obtain the value of what the company was once worth.

Jim agonized over the question: *What did his father do that he was not doing?* Jim felt the weight of a huge burden in letting his father down and failing his siblings.

His siblings were quick to criticize but slow to help. And when they did offer their help, Jim discounted their knowledge and abilities viewing them as more of a nuisance than a help. He also feared letting them see too closely just how far the business had deteriorated.

With no other options, Jim began secretly hunting for someone to buy the business. The only offer he received came not from a competitor, but from a land developer. This developer was offering Jim pennies on the dollar for what the business was worth. The developer intended to bulldoz   ant and turn it into a parking lot for the new mall he was building across the street.

In disgust, Jim thought, *Is this what my father's life work would become...a parking lot?* Surely his family deserved better than that, but he might not even have a family if he didn't do something—and quickly! What could Jim do to turn his business around? Was it too late? Was there still hope? Jim needed help!

For many entrepreneurs and business owners Jim's story is their story. Perhaps they find themselves working harder, longer, with less. Deep down they know they should be working on the root cause of problems and attending to strategic factors like values, vision and mission.

But they find themselves constantly rushing from one fire to the next. One day it's an equipment failure; the next day, it's a sexual harassment complaint in one of their departments; and the next day, it's their largest customer threatening to move to the competition.

All of this stress laps over into their family and social lives. They soon begin feeling like an outsider at home and tensions mount. In an attempt to self-medicate, unhealthy behaviors creep into their lives causing even more problems. So they "retreat" to work where all of this began.

They're frustrated and don't know where to turn for help. The frenzied pace at work numbs their senses and judgment and woos them into passivity. Yet, ironically, the business is ever and always on their minds.

Their business has become a ravenous beast that they're chained to. If they don't feed it constantly, it'll eat them alive.

WHY DO THEY FAIL?

Business leaders and organizations fail because they spend all of their time addressing the symptoms of the problem instead of its root causes. They focus on sales, marketing, production, strategy, cost-cutting, technology, etc. But they miss the root cause of their problems.

And what is the root cause of (and *solution* to) their problems? It's their *people*. People either make or break any organization. This begins with the leader. The leader of an organization may prove to be his/her own worst enemy. Poor leadership is the first reason that businesses fail.

General Electric leadership icon, Jack Welch said, "If you pick the right people and give them the opportunity to spread their wings and put compensation as a carrier behind it you almost don't have to manage them."

Conversely, you can pick the *wrong* people. Who are the wrong people? They are people who do not share the same values as you and your organization. They are people who do not have the best interests of your company at heart. They are people who were hired for a reason other than their ability and drive to see your organization succeed. But the onus falls on the leader who picked them.

Similarly, you can pick the right people, but deny them the opportunity to spread their wings. Does that sound too chaotic, too autonomous? If so, then you may be that leader who is too fearful, or too controlling to share the success of the organization. As Harry Truman said, "It's amazing what you can accomplish if you do not care who gets the credit."

Finally, you can pick the right people and give them the opportunity to spread their wings, but withhold reasonable financial incentives. The leader who functions in this manner communicates to his/her employees loud and clear that money is more important than they are.

Now, every business exists to make money, so this principle is counterintuitive. But when leaders value money above people, ultimately they will find themselves very lonely and without a business. Money alone is never a reason to exist. *Money is the reward for providing value to people.*

Listen to what Jack Welch is saying, because if we lead others the way he recommends, "You almost don't have to manage them." In other words, leading others in this manner becomes easy—a joy—rather than a burden. And a successful and profitable business results as a bi-product of such leadership.

A primary reason that businesses fail or aren't profitable is due to their leadership.

A second major reason that businesses fail results from hiring the wrong people, or putting the right people in the wrong positions. Think about your organization: what level of attention do you give to the human resource processes of recruiting, selection, compensation, training, and performance evaluation?

Many of these important human processes are flatly ignored or assigned to someone who has neither the experience nor position worthy of its demands. We give human resources lip service to satisfy compliance issues without ever intending to recognize its fundamental role in the business.

Another way we hire the wrong people is by hiring to skill and experience over values or character. Obviously, we want both character and skills. We want to hire people with integrity and whose values match those of our organization. And we want to hire those who have the skills to do the job.

The problem is that when both skill and character are not present, we always seem to let skill trump character. And inevitably, months or years later our poor choice comes back to bite us.

Most skills are easily trainable, whereas character is not. An employee who lacks character and the values of the organization will ultimately embarrass, undermine—or worse yet—influence other employees. "Bad company corrupts good character."[5]

As we will see, the carefully selected values of an organization must guide it through every business decision; serve as the compass by which the leader leads; and provide the standard for every personnel decision.

This brings us to the third major reason businesses collapse. *They fail to provide value, because they've failed in their values.* How tragic it is when a business breaks faith with its own stated values. But perhaps even more tragic is it when a business never even declares values.

When an organization does not establish clear values, they will invariably value money over people. And when they do, their fate is sealed—perhaps not immediately, but eventually.

Ironically, many businesses spend significant time and resources creating a set of values only to relegate them to a drawer somewhere. Oh, a new employee might have a brief brush with the company values in an hour-long orientation, only to find that he or she has entered "the real world" when they hit the floor.

I've already mentioned the great service that values provide us. In their most fundamental function they serve as the metrics by which we hold ourselves accountable and ensure integrity and responsibility in all areas.

Our business will rise or fall on our values and the extent to which we leverage their near infinite usefulness. Every business decision, every hire, every promotion, and everything we do should be guided by our values.

As leaders we owe it to our employees and all of our constituents to be able to say, "Our products and services may change; our location may change; the financial climate may change; but you can count on our values never changing."

In this chapter, we've taken a brief look at why businesses fail. We've focused on the three primary factors that lead to failure. In one way or another all three of these factors lead back to the primacy of people: the leader, our employees, and our values.

I hope this short review of the causes of failure has not discouraged you! In the chapters to come, we'll unpack each of these three themes: leadership, people and values in more detail and focus on how to build a growing thriving business!

Discussion Questions

1. In the Introduction, the author states, "Many CEOs and managers attempt to lead a *business* instead of leading *people*." What's the difference and why would this prove to be a fundamental flaw of business leadership?

2. The author also makes the claim, "Organizations that focus first on people have the best results." What companies can you think of fit this model? What companies fail miserably? How closely do you think their financial results are tied to their focus on people?

3. Explain in your own words why the author places so much importance on an organization's core values.

4. In Jim's story that opens chapter one, Jim's dad seems to be the consummate leader. And yet he appeared to neglect one key issue that led to the company's ultimate downfall. Apparently, he never coached or mentored his son. To what extent do you agree with this indictment against his leadership? How have you seen this issue played out in your experience?

5. Explain why the author identifies *people* as the real root cause of (and solution to) leaders' business problems.

6. Based on Jack Welch's statement below, in what ways can the leader be a cause of business failure? "If you pick the right people and give them the opportunity to spread their wings and put compensation as a carrier behind it you almost don't have to manage them."

7. Again, referring back to Jack Welch's quote and the author's explanation, in what ways can people (employees) be a significant factor in the failure of a business?

8. In what ways can the absence of values or failure to leverage them lead to a company's demise?

CHAPTER TWO

Seeking Solutions

Become brilliant at the basics.
– Vince Lombardi

In this chapter and the next one, I'd like to lay out before you my own journey in terms of what I'm calling, "The Leadership Code." The Leadership Code embraces both the "ingredients" *and* the techniques and skills a leader needs in order to build successful, well-running, world-class organizations.

In chapter one, you read Jim's story. I must now confess that that story was not fiction but played out within our family. It was my grandfather who had run the business so successfully for many years. Although I was attending college when the business began to decline, I was genuinely concerned for my uncle and his business. So much so, that I've devoted much of my professional career researching what factors lead to the success and failure of businesses.

In describing my journey in pursuit of The Leadership Code, I hope to provide you with many concrete examples and their contexts. As you will no doubt see, this is no armchair strategy, but one that has been born out of real life situations, with real people in real businesses.

BUILDING A GOOD FOUNDATION

Right out of university I took a job as a sales representative for a consumer packaged goods business in Canada. I had a lot of territory to cover, so that meant rising at 4:30am to be on the road by 5am and to the customer by 8am. My workdays were long, usually extending until 6 or 7pm after I had visited my last customer of the day. Drive, discipline and the fear of failure kept me on track.

Ken, my first boss was old school and had been in the consumer packaged goods business for decades. He was fair, honest, direct and to the point. He held high morals and strong values. Ken had developed and relied heavily on systems and he spent a lot of time training me in those systems.

I recall spending many -40C nights in hotels after a long day on the road. We'd eat supper at the hotel and then Ken would lead us in a two-hour training session—workbooks and all. I never felt I did very well in those sessions. I had my Honors Bachelors of Commerce degree, but that didn't seem to help at all in the real world.

Ken rarely complimented me, but he was fair, honest and direct. He always gave me the facts upfront and clearly told me where I needed to improve. He was never late for anything and was always the first one down for breakfast in the morning.

Ken's attention to detail and discipline were unbelievable. His morals, values and beliefs were consistent both in words and in actions. All of his sales reps (including me) admired and respected Ken whether we agreed with him or not.

Ken always presented himself in a way that matched his message. He dressed conservatively but sharply, with everything clean and pressed, shoes always shined. Ken had routines that he adhered to meticulously that we needed to follow to be successful sales reps. If I thought I had found a better way to do something, I had to make sure that I had all my facts together and vetted before he would even consider a possible change. As far as he was concerned, his processes were tried and true.

One of Ken's training processes seemed harsh to me at the time, but the message it sent was loud and clear. When new sales reps had been training with Ken for six months, he would indiscriminately question and refuse a number of our business expenses we submitted each week.

Because this system had worked for him over the years he would refuse an expense no matter how legitimate it seemed. The message he wanted to send all new sales reps was that he read all expense reports. So we'd better not try to submit an expense for something that was not covered by company policy.

I never cheated on my expense reports and never even considered doing so. Therefore, when he refused a $6 charge from McDonald's for my dinner, I was blown away! I thought if I could explain it to him he would understand and approve it. I believed that I had an ironclad case.

You see, my sales car had broken down in a small, remote city and wouldn't be repaired until afternoon the following day. Ken could not have me just sitting at the hotel watching TV all day, so he told me to rent a car and complete my route the next day, then return the rental and pick up my sales car and drive home.

This was no easy task since it required me to get up very early in the morning to go to my first stop about three hours away. Then I had to drive another two-and-a-half hours north to call on my customers there and then back-track to pick up my car. All totaled this was over 10 hours of driving not including sales calls!

At the end of the day, after picking up my sales car, the drive home was another 6 or 7 hours. So, I stopped at McDonalds for some food to eat in the car on my long drive home. I finally reached home after midnight.

Obviously, I felt my case was solid, but Ken refused me the reimbursement on principle. The company's policy clearly stated that on the day a sales rep arrived home he/she should be home for supper. Therefore, per company policy, Ken would not authorize the expense.

Wow, I was shocked! But I did get over it and Ken's leadership style taught me some valuable lessons:

1. *Measure it to manage it.* All reports must have meaning and managers must read them and provide feedback on them. This principle ensures that accuracy and performance will improve, because the employee knows that these things are measured and matter. (I later found out that this is a proven principle called the Hawthorne Effect.)

2. *Back up what you say with your actions.* If you want to earn respect and be treated with respect by your employees, you need to adhere to the standards you enforce and dress the part. My dad, who was an athletic coach,

always said, "You need to dress sharp to play sharp." His teams were always very successful, but if a team member showed up with the wrong colored socks to a game he would not let him play.

3. *Lead with discipline and direct, straight forward direction.* This promotes high standards and engenders the respect of the employees. Ken always addressed issues head on and never beat around the bush or let things slide with his employees. He always held all of us to a very high standard.

4. *Provide cutting-edge training and always train better than your competition.* The training that the company provided me was even better than our much larger competitors. The company gave us the tools and training to be the best. Since then, I've always tried to do the same.

5. *Value employees and their spouses or partners.* When I worked for Ken, my wife (girlfriend at the time) and I lived an eight-hour drive from the head office. The company invited her to join me at the company Christmas party. They flew us in, put us up in the hotel for two nights, (and paid for two separate rooms) and flew us back. That experience showed me how much the company cared about me and my life and demonstrated their values as a company. It made those long days and hard work so much more bearable.

    As soon as I became a manager I incorporated this practice for every team I managed whether it was company policy or not. And I always found a way to save money in the budget to pay for it. This was a signature of my leadership style and gave me the opportunity to meet all of the significant others and thank them for allowing their partners to put in extra time when they needed to.

After working for Ken as a sales rep, I was promoted to Key Account Manager and assigned to Gord, my new boss. Gord had been in the business for many years and sales was what he knew.

At the time I was one of the first University graduates that the company had hired for sales in Western Canada. Although Gord had no post-secondary education he was very good at his job and was the classic mentor/teacher.

By now I was very comfortable with my role in the company and had just set several sales records in my territory. Ironically, that was the territory that Gord had last held and I had been hired to replace him when he was promoted to another region. So needless to say, Gord could have been easily intimidated, jealous, or even envious of my success.

Gord was anything but those things! He did everything in his power to train me, promote me, write letters on my behalf, give me awards, and stand up in meetings and tell top management about my newest achievements.

Gord was truly self-effacing when it came to putting his best employees forward. Gord was very confident in his position, but built me up to believe that I may someday be his boss. At first, I felt uncomfortable when he told me this and I don't think I understood his motives or the reality of what he was saying. In my mind at the time, Gord was my boss!

Here's some of what I learned from Gord:

1. *Be a teacher, mentor and role model for your employees.* I believe that good leadership is more caught than taught. We need to model and coach for our employees what we want them to become.

    Share with your employees everything you know that took years to develop and acquire. Invest in them so that they'll be sharper, smarter and more talented than you are. This is crucial to becoming a great manager and leader and will evoke complete trust on the part of your employees.

2. *Give credit to your employees and promote them whenever possible.* As I learned from Gord, I often told my star direct reports that I would be proud to work for them someday.

3. *Communicate and demonstrate that you have your employees' best interests at heart.* This builds trust that will reward you with loyal, hard-working employees. It also serves you well when you have to have those tough conversations and let someone go.

    Because of the trust that you have built up and the candid and direct communication you have had over time with the employee, the day you need to let them go is not a big surprise for them. They know that you are letting them go not only because it's best for the company, but also because it's what's best for them.

    They understand that this wasn't a good fit and they need to find a position that better matches their capabilities. This ultimately reduces their stress and yours.

After serving in that capacity for some time under Gord, another firm acquired our company and replaced many of our management team with their own managers. The two years following the takeover were hellish.

All of Western Canada was consolidated into a new region and our new Regional Manager was brought in from the outside. Bob (not his real name) became my boss. Ken had retired, but Bob fired Gord for no other reason than Gord challenged him on some things. I believe the only reason I was not fired during this period was that I had developed a great relationship with Bob's boss, Mike.

Mike, a manager with the acquiring company, had become Bob's boss. I picked Mike up at the airport one day and he informed me that he was promoting me to Sr. Key Account Manager responsible for all major accounts in Western Canada. This was an unexpected and huge promotion and he and I bonded from that day forward.

However, Bob's management style threw our region back into the Dark Ages:

- Bob never shared any information with us.
- When he was in the office he kept his door shut.
- We never knew where we stood with him.
- He routinely waited till the last minute and piled work on us Friday afternoon requiring its completion by Sunday evening.
- Bob was the antithesis of good leadership.

During Bob's management I learned the valuable lesson of building a strong relationship with my boss' boss. I learned a lot from Mike.

Eventually, the company recognized Bob's incompetency and fired him. Mike replaced Bob by promoting me to Regional Manager for Western Canada, so I reported directly to him.

Here are some of the valuable lessons I learned from Mike:

1. *Include your top employees in the high-level decision-making process of the company.* Mike took a liking to me and included me in all of the headquarter meetings in Toronto. He valued my knowledge with our products and my relationships with our customers. He called me an "A" employee, listened to everything I said, and gave me as much responsibility as I could handle.

2. *Do all you can to minimize corporate red tape and remove barriers for your employees.* Mike constantly did this for me, making my job easier and building loyalty.

3. *Work hard and play hard.* Mike expected nothing but the best from us and he rewarded us with meals at nice restaurants and retreats at beautiful getaways.

4. *Leverage social times and off-site meetings to deepen relationships with employees.* Mike was a big believer in off-site meetings and going to dinner together while traveling. In this way, he got to know his employees more personally and in environments that cultivated true bonding and teamwork.

These deepened relationships paid huge dividends back in the office as we were more trusting, less guarded, and could conduct very candid discussions.

As the new Regional Manager, the first thing I did was assemble my team. The team I had inherited had been battered and over-worked without reward or praise for the past two years. Their trust had been completely destroyed.

I was now managing my former peers. Because I already knew my team, I had a pretty good idea who would stay and who I needed to let go.

Some left simply because they couldn't see reporting to someone who had been below them prior to this. With others, I conducted tough discussions about their future and that what we had in mind would not be a good fit for them. With those open positions, I then targeted the best in the industry to fill key roles.

As soon as I had my team assembled, I booked an offsite meeting in which I hoped to build trust and infuse the team with energy and high morale. Also, many on the team had never worked for me and did not know my management style. And with new team players on board, the whole team needed time to get to know each other.

For the offsite, I booked an island resort off the coast of Vancouver, British Columbia that we had to fly into by float plane. I kept it a surprise until we boarded the float plane. This single three-day meeting and bonding session developed one of the most productive and cohesive teams I've ever had the privilege to be a part of.

We became like a family and everyone respected and trusted everyone else fully. Every team member felt the need to be engaged and came up with unbelievable solutions to our challenges.

Following that initial offsite, I let a different provincial manager host our quarterly meetings. This engendered a healthy competition as each manager tried to outdo the last. This friendly competition spilled over into our meetings and in the evening when we challenged each other to a game of basketball, volleyball, floor hockey, or paintball. We always did something together like this for "bragging rights" and to cultivate deep relationships and trust.

Also, I found it vital to keep work teams intact in these competitions. There's no sense in conducting teambuilding exercises for an interdepartmental team that never works together. Each work team found it tremendously valuable to play together in this way, deepening relationships and establishing camaraderie.

Let me fine-tune what I just said, because I also learned the hard way to never confuse or blend business relationships and personal relationships. In other words, business relationships are maintained in the business setting and personal relationships are reserved for non-business settings.

In the business setting I wear my business "hat" and have complete freedom to speak with my employees about any and all business issues. So any personal relationship I have with them does not improperly influence my business relationship with them.

Our team was so successful in the business that we rose from dead-last to first place. We were awarded the prestigious President's Award. In keeping with what Ken, Gord and Mike had taught me, I rewarded my team and their spouses with a weekend at the luxurious Banff Springs Hotel in the Canadian Rockies.

My team continued its success each and every year growing our business by double-digits in categories that were supposedly in decline. The Banff trip became something we all aspired to each year. The spouses loved it as well and frequently asked, "Are we going to Banff this year?" Every year we set targets for ourselves that would warrant such a trip.

These trips not only served as a reward for stellar performance, they also provided an intimate setting in which the management team got to know each other and their spouses. Our love for and enjoyment of each other was authentic. The off-sites and annual all-inclusive retreats played a critical role in building the success then and in all the future teams I managed.

Over the years I've been a part of other similar events that were not successful. Some of the factors that I believe *derail* team development include:

- The off-site is held at the home office or somewhere else not conducive to openness and sharing.
- The off-site is so close to the employees' homes that they go home at night and miss out on the after-hours teambuilding.
- The lead manager fails to provide a non-work, team-building opportunity in the evenings.
- If teambuilding opportunities are present, natural work teams are split up so that the exercise is conducted with people you won't normally work with.
- The spirit of the off-site is counter to what the team experiences on a daily basis, making it feel contrived and phony.
- The leader is the first one to bed at night.

Obviously, the kinds of off-site events I'm talking about here involve a lot of planning and preparation. I could have merely showered my team members with gifts or thrown money at them for a fun getaway, but I wanted to leverage our time away so that it paid dividends all year long.

Discussion Questions

1. The author tells about his first boss, Ken and his refusal to authorize a $6 meal from McDonalds. What do you think about how Ken handled that situation? How might you have handled it differently and why? If you had been AJ's boss and had authorized his meal, what lessons might this young sales rep have learned from that?

2. Discuss the lesson, *Measure it to manage it* that the author lists as a result of working for Ken. To what extent is this principle followed in your company? How important is it to you and why? In what ways could you implement this principle to a greater extent in your organization?

3. Another principle gleaned from Ken's leadership says, *provide cutting-edge training and always train better than your competition.* How would you rank your organization in this regard? What training have you received since joining the organization? How can you improve the training in your company?

4. Select one of the three principles that the author learned from his bosses. Discuss how well your company follows this principle and how it could improve.

5. From his bosses, the author learned the value of off-sites and an annual celebration including spouses for building morale and teamwork. Express why you think this practice is so valuable.

6. If you were to plan an off-site meeting for your direct reports for the purpose of strategy and teambuilding, what elements would you include?

7. Think of the best boss you've ever worked for. What lessons did you learn from him/her?

CHAPTER THREE

Putting The Leadership Code to the Test

It takes the same energy to think small as it does to think big.
So dream big and think bigger.
– Daymond John

As you can see from my story so far, I started out early in my career doing many of the things my grandfather did that I felt were crucial to his success. Additionally, with every new boss I worked for, I gleaned practices and principles that would serve me well as I led others in business.

Working as a Regional Manager, I had the additional challenge of leading a team that was spread out across the country—from Thunder Bay, Ontario, to Victoria, British Columbia. As I spent time with my sales reps, I discovered that they often held entirely different views of our company vision, mission and goals than what we wished to communicate.

This taught me that as a manager, it's easy to assume that your whole team is on the same page and that we're all pulling in the same direction. But the farther away your employees are from the source, the weaker and more confused the message becomes.

If you ever played the telephone game as a kid, you've experienced the degradation of the message as it's passed from one person to the next around the room. At the end of the game when you compare the message that the last person heard with the original message communicated, the two messages are often not even remotely similar.

My point here is that while the distance between the manager and their employees increases, so does the need to spend time with them ensuring that they fully understand the goals and vision. Don't assume anything.

Let me summarize some of those practices and principles that I've covered so far:

- I made it a priority to "Walk the floor" (or travel to their locations) to meet with and know my employees, no matter what level they were in the organization.

- I ensured that everyone on our team knew what we needed to accomplish and where we were going as a group. Everyone clearly knew what was expected of them.

- I always treated our employees well and respected their time and their families. All of our major planning meetings were at nice locations off-site and I made sure they were well taken cared for. We always found savings to pay for these and justified them as a reward for our performance.

- I recognized the sacrifices employees made in their personal lives and I include their partners in that recognition. The intent was to clearly communicate and thank the spouses and partners for their part in making our company successful. I wanted to thank them for the sacrifices they had to make during the year due to the extra hours their partner put in.

※ Over the 15-plus-years of my career to that point, I continued to hone my skills and experiment with building a world class organization.

※ I researched the topic of leadership and business success extensively and implemented and tweaked many of the processes in order to come up with the best outcomes.

It was at this point in my career that I was given an amazing opportunity to battle test all that I had learned from my grandfather, past bosses, research and experience. The organization I worked for gave me the assignment to build and staff a brand new Contact Center on Cyprus in the Mediterranean.

We had a small contact center operation in London, but the company decided to move it to Cyprus. Initially, the Cyprus operation consisted of just two employees from accounting. The new contact center would also include the fraud and collusion department, electronic payment processing and payroll.

On the one hand, I had several advantages going into this project. For one, the subsidiary was far away from the corporate office, so that we were not under close scrutiny and the strict controls of corporate guidelines. This provided the perfect incubator to test and retest my ideas, systems and programs.

Also, there are obvious advantages to a green startup. There were no entrenched employees, negative mindsets, or poor past practices that I had to purge before building the contact center.

On the other hand, I faced some formidable obstacles in setting up this contact center. First, being situated on a small island, the potential employee base was very limited. Added to that, we needed to provide 24/7 customer support in 12 languages using four different formats: call-ins, emails, chat, and call backs. This meant that 70 percent of the workforce had to be brought in from outside the country.

Finally, the idyllic location on an island in the Mediterranean challenged us with its four S's: sun, sand, sea and sex. We had no problem attracting employees to our location, but the ever-present siren song of the four S's threatened to lure employees from the contact center and from their duties once they arrived there.

In our first year of operation, we were running over 100 percent turnover! We could not hire fast enough in order to fill the empty chairs. There are hefty financial, productivity, and morale costs associated with high turnover.

Nevertheless, in three years, we took a two person operation to an organization employing over 120 people. Within four years of launching, we had drastically reduced our turnover rate to just four percent—an enviable rate in any industry.

We achieved the following metrics in the two top-box scores: our employee satisfaction ranked over 90 percent; customer satisfaction over 88 percent; our overall quality score 98 percent; and our first contact resolution over 85 percent. Many of these measures were validated by a third-party audit.

Starting from scratch, we turned the division into a world class operation in four to five years, winning the best Contact Center in the World under 50 seats. This was a global award and one of the most prestigious awards at the Contact Center World event held in Las Vegas. We also received a silver medal for the best recruitment campaign.

As we started out, I looked at the things I had already learned in my career. I had been able to turn divisions around from being the worst to the best. We produced extraordinary results and were recognized as "best in the world."

We had achieved that level of success and status by following a simple leadership code that works every time. The solution to our primary problems in business is people. Nothing works unless you get the people right and develop an environment for them to flourish.

Here's what I've observed:

- Departments or organizations that focus on people first achieve the best results.
- Without the right people, leadership and environment all other solutions seem to fail.
- The more time we spend on the people management process, the better the results we deliver and the less stress and time is required.
- It all comes down to values and people. With great people and strong aligned values anything is possible!
- The solution is to identify, assess, train and motivate those people into producing extraordinary results.
- Some organizations have the right *ingredients* to be the best, but they fail for reasons we'll discuss later.

In the chapters that follow, we'll take a closer look at each of the key factors of The Leadership Code: leadership, people and core values. This Leadership Code has worked for me time and time again and was developed over nearly 30 years of management experience. I am convinced it will work for you too.

THE LEADERSHIP CODE

The Leadership Code consists of three primary elements: *leadership, people* and *values.* We can view these in terms of the "ingredients" in the bread-making analogy. Many organizations possess the ingredients for success, but relatively few blend them in a way that achieves perpetual stellar success.

One of the keys to blending these ingredients in practice is to view them as fully integrated with each other. Often, in our effort to break things down into teachable and manageable chunks, we isolate the pieces and fail to see their relationship and interdependency with the other pieces.

Or worse yet, we pick and choose which elements we'll focus on to the neglect of the others. None of these three elements: *leadership, people* and *values* can be practiced in isolation from the others.

For this reason, as we work through each of these three elements, I will constantly show how each blends with the others.

Also, I have listed the three elements in a *logical* order, but not necessarily a *chronological* one. Depending on your situation, certain processes may follow a chronological order, but ultimately they all must blend.

Finally, I believe that successful business leadership is a honed, professional expertise that requires years of training, failing, and practice in order to become proficient. Within any organization and its current situation are innumerable factors that require a broad spectrum of abilities on the part of a great leader.

In reality, there are very many things that a leader must learn to do well. Also, whenever we are dealing with people, no matter how disciplined we are, there will always be a certain amount of messiness and unpredictability involved. All of this may seem overwhelming to the leader, but I suppose it's no different than learning any other skilled craft.

For this reason, we will attempt to look at the full spectrum of all that a leader must be and do to take an organization to become a thriving and highly motivated world class organization, producing effortless growth and profits year after year.

Discussion Questions

1. The author comments, "I made it a priority to 'Walk the floor' and know my employees." What does this practice look like? When did you experience this practice from a boss? When have you put this into practice as a manager?

2. Another of AJ's principles in this chapter says, "I ensured that everyone on our team knew what we needed to accomplish and where we were going as a group. Everyone clearly knew what was expected of them." Discuss why there is often such a big gap between knowing this and putting it into practice.

3. Assess your current practice of researching and honing your leadership/management skills. What habits and goals would you like to put into place to ensure that you are a better leader tomorrow than you are today?

4. The author claims, "Departments or organizations that focus on people first achieve the best results." To what extent do you buy into this claim? Where have you seen it demonstrated?

5. AJ insists, "The solution is to identify, assess, train and motivate those people into producing extraordinary results." How much time and attention does your organization typically spend on these elements? How is that working out?

CHAPTER FOUR

Leadership

My main job was developing talent. I was a gardener providing water and other nourishment to our top 750 people. Of course, I had to pull out some weeds, too.
— Jack Welch

ATTRIBUTES OF A GREAT LEADER

The role of a winning leader is to work oneself out of a job. I mean that facetiously, of course, because such a leader will always be in high demand. However, if as a leader you want to see your organization excel, you must help your employees excel.

The outstanding leader constantly seeks to help their people grow and learn so that they can one day out-perform the leader. I had the privilege of seeing this come about at the Contact Center. After I had retired, leaving one of my former lieutenants in charge, he called me back sometime later to work for him as a consultant.

Working oneself out of a job requires selfless behavior, integrity, humility and a genuine desire to empower others that is rare. These character traits don't come easy and they're difficult to maintain. They require constant attention, reflection, correction and recalibration. Our employees serve as the best mirror to reflect how well we are leading.

Following are some of the characteristics of great teachers and mentors. They must:

- Ask great open-ended questions
- Listen actively
- Be secure in their own position, not feeling threatened should a subordinate surpass their teacher
- Model the skills and principles they seek to impart (practice what they preach)
- Maintain consistency and predictability over the long-haul
- Demonstrate a high level of emotional and relational intelligence
- Appreciate the unique talents, skills and personality of their mentees, not trying to clone themselves
- Challenge their employees boldly, honestly and clearly
- Give praise and recognition freely

WINNING LEADERS PUT PEOPLE FIRST

Putting people first is what we often refer to as "servant leadership." The leader must unselfishly recognize that the only way to accomplish the organization's goals is by genuinely serving others. In fact, when I sat down with employees to explain what my organization looked like and how it functioned, I'd show them an inverted pyramid with me at the bottom and the employees at the top.

Using this upside-down pyramid, I would emphasize that my primary purpose was to remove obstacles and barriers to great performance. After all, it is the first-line employees who engage daily with our customers—not me. We need to treat our employees like we want them to treat our best customers.

Putting people first also means that as a leader you own the people development process. Leaders often try to pawn this off on the human resource department, merely paying it lip service.

I constantly evaluate my own leadership in terms of putting people first by asking the following questions:

Am I spending enough time getting to know my employees?

I have seen time and again that the more time we invest into our people, the more productive our organization will be. Spending time with our employees is not only a more humane approach to leading, it is also more productive.

Personally getting to know our employees is crucial for building trust. I made it a habit to walk the floor every day. In my opinion, spending any less than 50 percent of our time with our employees is too little. Set appointments over the year, so you can have at least one sit-down meeting with each employee who has been with your company for a year.

By spending time with our employees we gain a better understanding of their challenges, joys and skills. In his book, *Good to Great,* Jim Collins speaks of the importance of having people in the "right seat on the bus." How can we possibly assess that vital issue without knowing our employees?

Create opportunities for meeting with larger groups of employees regularly through: Coffee with the CEO, town hall meetings, and fireside chats. Let them ask questions and speak with them freely about the business. Use these public meetings to provide encouragement and recognition.

Get to know your employees' spouses or partners as well. Stop in and just talk with your employees. Show them through your actions that you really care.

Spending time with employees goes against the grain of what most leaders think they need to be about. I'm sure many reading this are probably thinking, "There's no way I can afford to spend that kind of time with my employees!"

But the opposite is true. If you don't invest this time in people, you will eventually become overwhelmed. Either you must invest in others, or all responsibility comes back on you. Without truly engaging the minds and skills of others, you're creating an organization that "can't even tie its shoe" without your input. Everyone and everything will be dependent on you.

Leaders who build their organizations around them with a high level of dependency are self-absorbed, fearful, and insecure. No one has the capacity to carry that burden for long. The organization, its employees and the leader will suffer and pay dearly for it.

Conversely, the more time you put into your people, the more productive your organization will become and the more time you'll have to enjoy its fruits. I believe that spending time with people is the most critical part of becoming a successful organization and there are no shortcuts.

How well do my employees understand the values of the organization?

Your organization's core values are foundational for everything you do. Values don't necessarily describe *what* you do (your product or service), but values provide the context for *how* you do what you do.

Core values represent the *standard* that you've agreed to abide by. The core values provide a *compass* to keep you and your organization on track. This is incredibly freeing for the organization. Operating by a clear set of core values prevents rogue or rash actions, replacing those with predictability and reliability.

Every aspect of the business should be filtered through the values. Your core values should be front and center at all times in your organization, never leaving employees wondering about what to expect or how to handle difficult situations.

Above all, you as a leader must live and breathe your organization's core values. The core values will only be important to others if they are important to you. Ignore or violate the core values and they become meaningless jingles printed on a coffee mug.

All personnel decisions, performance reviews, and compensation should be tied to your core values. Make this so obvious that all employees know exactly what's expected of them, how and why. We tied 50 percent of employees' evaluation to the core values and the other 50 percent to performance.

I will spend a lot more time on this matter in the chapter on values.

To what extent am I shouldering my responsibility for achieving both short- and long-term objectives?

This is where many leaders roll up their sleeves, grit their teeth and say, "Yes, this is what I'm designed for." But let me return to what I said earlier. As a leader, the primary means for fulfilling our responsibilities and achieving results is through other people. We must spend time with our employees.

Don't mistake this for mere glad-handing fluff! As we get to know our employees, we find out what their personal and corporate goals are. We discover their aspirations; what they are really good at; and what they're passionate about.

Then we provide opportunities for them to channel all their energies into the success of the business. We don't let up on this. Just because we spend a lot of time with them getting to know them doesn't mean that we're going to let things slide. We hold them accountable.

When executed properly, this combination of relationship building and high expectations brings huge results. This is why people development and ensuring that the right people are in the right jobs is so important to the success of the organization.

Our employees know they can trust us to make tough decisions and that we will carry them out as humanely as possible. By the same token, our main concern is not whether we are liked by our employees, but whether we are *respected* by them. Respect comes as the reward of trust.

Our role is to guide, critique, coach and mentor people to improve their performance. We've got to make sure that everyone understands and follows our values, vision, mission and goals.

We must nip "red light thinking" and negativism (or complaints without solutions) in the bud before it spreads like cancer throughout the organization. In all of this it helps to remind ourselves that we are leading *people* rather than an inanimate *company.*

What am I doing that frustrates my employees?

This is a crucial question for me, because when employees are frustrated they are distracted from what we're paying them to do. Frustration breeds discontent, anger, fear, poor morale and lack of productivity.

Far be it from us as leaders that we should ever frustrate our employees deliberately. I had such a boss for two years. He took delight in making our lives miserable. The organization and its people suffered under his capricious leadership by every measure imaginable. The company finally invited him to take his management style elsewhere.

Respect for one another (however you choose to express it) should be a core value of any organization. We kill trust and respect as leaders when we fail to be responsive to our employees. I set a standard for myself by responding within 24 hours of a request or question. I do this no matter who it is from, and if I can't answer it right away, I give the employee a time frame by which I will follow up.

Someone has said that we should treat our employees in the manner in which we would like them to treat our best customers.

Other ways we can frustrate employees and show them disrespect includes:

※ Canceling meetings at the last minute demonstrates poor planning on our part and ignores their time and schedules.

※ Reprimanding them in front of their peers humiliates the employee and undermines our leadership.

※ Changing our mind frequently saps our employees of the confidence and direction they seek from us.

※ Not clarifying expectations represents a huge de-motivator for our employees and will get us into trouble, costing the organization time, money and trust.

※ Focusing on superficial rather than substantial matters detracts and distracts from what's important.

※ Assigning work and then micro-managing employees robs them of the autonomy and empowerment they desire and flourish under. When we assign work, we must make sure we know the capabilities of the person to whom we're assigning it. Give employees room and permission to fail.

※ Not listening to employees demonstrates that we don't care what they have to say. Instead, practice active listening skills and model for them what this looks like.

※ Not recognizing their achievements devalues their work and will ultimately undermine performance. Be careful not to dilute recognition, thereby making it meaningless.

※ Communicating that we already know it all...will stifle creativity and participation from others. Instead, rely on their individual areas of expertise, their input and ideas.

※ By being moody we put our employees on guard and we set the tone for the organization. Always present a positive, friendly attitude. You have a smile, use it!

How well have I established a clear direction for the organization? And to what extent do my employees feel engaged in the work, knowing that their ideas matter?

Apart from a people-first mentality, the leader can get caught up in their own little world. The leader may know where the organization is heading, but has not communicated that throughout the organization.

Zig Ziglar said, "Research indicates that employees have three prime needs: Interesting work, recognition for doing a good job, and being let in on things that are going on in the company."

Employees want to be a part of something bigger than they are. They need to see the big picture. They desire to know how they can play a vital role in the success of the organization.

We must explain to the whole organization the how, why and what we are doing. Keeping people in the dark only produces mediocre energy focused toward poorly perceived objectives.

Town hall meetings can provide an appropriate and productive platform for communicating the goals and direction of your organization. Town hall meetings require two-way communication and offer a great venue for employees to make an impact on the organization.

In one town hall meeting, I remember Steve, a new employee, who was not afraid to ask tough questions. This was the first time I had engaged with him in this context. Based on his questions, I could tell he was a winner, so we began to track and develop him.

Steve eventually moved to the top of the organization and became the best Contact Center Manager we ever had. By rewarding Steve's behavior, the other employees began behaving in the same way.

If among the rank and file employees you begin hearing "them-and-us" talk ("them" referring to the head office), you know you are not providing sufficient direction and communication to your employees.

Grasp every opportunity to upgrade your team, using every encounter as a means for evaluating, coaching, and building confidence in your employees. Ask employees, "How can I remove obstacles that prevent great performance?"

How clearly have I communicated about business goals and their performance?

This is similar to the previous question, but more focused. Always over-communicate about the goals of the organization. Every employee must know what is expected of them, by when and to what standard. Look for ways to do this that are easy to grasp and are fun.

As Vice President of Business Development at the head office, we had a product that all the employees thought we were better at than anyone else. But healthy market share is a true scorecard of that measure. So we designed a mural of a horse track and assigned a horse to each of our competitors. We placed each horse on the track based on that competitor's market share. Our horse was dead last!

When the employees saw how far back in the race we actually were, they finally got it and saw how far we had to improve to get into first place. This graphic changed the culture from lackadaisical to one of competitive urgency.

Each quarter, we moved the position of the horses to signify each competitor's standing with respect to ours. Our organization worked very hard to get our horse to the front of the pack.

In terms of performance, we also must have the confidence to make unpopular decisions separating business from personal relationships. Ask questions with curiosity and skepticism. Do not let things slide. Constantly drive for better understanding.

- Follow up and hold people accountable. Follow-up is vital for achieving respect and discipline in the organization. Know when to celebrate successes with your team and your direct reports no matter how big or small. And apply the appropriate recognition.

- Inspire and reward fact-based, calculated risk and loss. Don't be quick to blame. Instead, shoulder the responsibility of authorized decisions that failed. Don't send emails when you have an issue with an employee, but handle issues face-to-face.

- I let my employees know that I don't like surprises. If they have bad news to tell me, I want to hear it now, not later. We may be able to solve a problem now, or prevent it from growing worse.

- I give my employees the same courtesy. I do not procrastinate with bad news. I want to squelch rumors before they even surface. I want people to know they can always come to me for direct answers to their questions.

≉ I also let employees know that I will not accept second best and neither should they. Let them feel your drive to succeed and communicate up front that you will not tolerate passive employees. Employees who are failing to grow must go. Emphasize, encourage and reward continuous learning and development.

Tom Peters advises, "Give a lot, expect a lot, and if you don't get it, prune."

To what extent am I paying attention to my leadership style?

As mentioned before, leaders gravitate toward one or the other end of the leadership spectrum. One extreme is direct leadership and the other is consensus leadership. The following table shows the contrasting elements of both style extremes:

Direct Leadership	Consensus Leadership
• There is no discussion and no debate	• There is plenty of discussion and input by all
• The leader is in control and makes all decisions	• The team makes decisions
• Things are urgent and the pace quick	• There is no pressure to come up with an immediate solution
• This style is required in a crisis or emergency	• Everyone's concerns are dealt with to come up with a proposed solution
• This is a short-term, temporary leadership style • This would be used in the military in a combat situation	• This is most appropriate for brainstorming ideas and solutions when time and opportunity permit

The danger for any leader is to default to one or the other extreme, or to apply a style that is inappropriate for a given scenario. When a leader gets stuck in one style, they will fail.

Leaders must learn to work well in both extremes and everywhere in-between. We do this by assessing each situation and applying the right amount of leadership for that moment.

Tom Peters adds to this focus to leadership, "Leaders don't create followers, they create more leaders." With this emphasis, we constantly adjust our leadership style to leverage a situation to the benefit of the individual employee *and* the organization.

Discussion Questions

1. What do you think of the concept of leading to work your-self out of a job?

2. How much time do your regularly spend getting to know your employees? How is that working? What will you keep doing or do differently?

3. According to the author, what role do values play in an organization? What role do they play in yours?

4. What is the connection between a people-first mentality and taking full responsibility for the short- and long-term goals of the organization?

5. In what ways has a current or former boss frustrated you? In what ways might you be frustrating employees right now? What will you do differently?

6. How well do your employees understand business goals and what's expected of them? On a scale of 1 to 5, 1 being low, how would you score your performance in this area?

7. Between the two leadership style extremes of direct leadership and consensus leadership, which are you more prone to default to? What are the results of each style? When is each style appropriate and when is it not? Brainstorm some ways to break out of that tendency.

CHAPTER FIVE

People First: Recruitment

Excellent teams are built around individual excellence.
– Marcus Buckingham & Curt Coffman

Your people—the people you recruit, hire, train and lead—will either bring about the success of your organization or be the root cause of its failure. People are the key to the growth and prosperity of your company.

True competitive advantage comes from its people. How they perform cannot be easily copied. Your people are your most important non-replicated resource. If you want to provide world-class operating results and customer service, then you must focus on your people.

I like to look at The Leadership Code in terms of a bicycle wheel. I see the organization's values as the hub of the wheel. From the values, come alignment, power and synchronized work. People are the spokes. They become extensions of the hub driving the wheel.

If you've ever ridden a bicycle and a spoke breaks or becomes slack, it throws the whole wheel (organization) off kilter. The wheel begins to wobble and cannot operate at speed. Its wobble begins to rub within the frame causing friction. This also places undue stress on the neighboring spokes.

But when all the spokes are in place and doing what they're designed to do, the wheel turns easily and smoothly. People are energized to be a part of something much bigger than them. They enjoy seeing the organization move forward swiftly, smoothly and with efficiency.

Consider briefly what motivates employees to either leave an organization or stay. In my experience, employees leave an organization for the following key reasons:

- Misalignment between expectations and actual work
- The job doesn't fit them
- The boss offers insufficient feedback and coaching
- Career opportunities are limited, not valued, or not well paid
- Life work imbalance
- Loss of trust and confidence in senior management
- Poor supervisors
- Low salaries
- Poor working conditions
- Lack of training and growth opportunities

Similarly, employees tend to remain with an organization when they:

- Have an emotional commitment and sense of connection to the firm's mission and vision
- Know what is expected of them at work
- Possess the materials and equipment needed to do their job
- Have the opportunity to do their best every day
- Experience a positive, fun work environment
- Receive recognition and praise for doing good work every week
- Are cared for by their boss
- Experience encouragement from their boss to continue their personal development

Because people are so vital to the success of any organization, we cannot take the above issues for granted. We must give very deliberate and special attention to the practices of: recruitment and hiring, training and development, leading and performance management. For the remainder of the book, we'll look at each of these practices.

RECRUITMENT

In recruiting potential employees we must be very clear about what we're looking for and potential employees must see a clear picture of what we are recruiting them to. Although we haven't talked about them at length yet, your organization's values are basic to what we're referring to here.

Many organizations post a job merely in search of a skill-set. But if an organization hires an individual whose values don't align with that organization, that employee's skill-set is practically unimportant. The candidate whose values do not align with those of the organization will never last.

Within The Leadership Code, what we are looking for in an employee are four things: talent, skills, knowledge, and values.

- **Talent** is not something you can teach. Talent is hardwired into an individual. Talents are unique to an individual. For instance, a candidate may have a talent for building relationships and teams—something that the position you're hiring for may not currently require. But having those skills may set that candidate head and shoulders above other candidates with like skills and experience.

- **Skills** can be taught. Granted, if you're hiring someone to perform electrical engineering, you'll want someone who already possesses those skills, or at least a certain level of those skills. More importantly: does this individual have the ability to learn and are they teachable?

- **Knowledge** is what a candidate has gained through training and experience. This can be verified through background and reference checks, testing, and demonstration.

- **Values** that align with those of your organization are vital. While some values can be learned, others are the product of an individual's upbringing and character. For example, an individual who possesses the talents, skills and knowledge for a position but lacks integrity or respect for others would be eliminated from the pool of candidates. Values are crucial and we'll spend more time on them later in this book.

Part of recruitment means having a great selection process in place for screening and interviewing candidates. A "people-first" focus starts here. Candidates need to feel that the selection process is fair, respectful and meaningful. That is—every candidate is treated equitably, with respect, in a timely fashion and in a way that is relevant to the job for which they are applying.

Your selection process should radiate your organization's values. In any one phase of the process, candidates should walk away thinking, "I'd really like to work with those people." Or, at the very least, "I see that this job is not a good fit for me, but I'd highly recommend this company to other job seekers."

INTERVIEWING

A good selection process is built like a funnel with a broad beginning, ever narrowing down to the final phase of hiring. We won't go into the details of such a selection funnel, but it generally begins with screening a resume, filling out an application, followed by a phone interview, followed by one or more face-to-face interviews that may include testing or demonstration through a simulation.

We always narrowed the funnel down to a handful of candidates for what I call "deep dive" interviews. Then I would rotate my senior managers through to interview them too. In this way, I was able to get more than just my own opinion.

I always had at least three interviewers, which increased the odds of finding the right candidate the first time. One of those interviewers was always my HR person. After completing the interviews, all of us who interviewed the candidates met in a room and compared our notes, discussing the pros and cons of each candidate.

Then we force-ranked the candidates to reduce the candidate pool to just one or two candidates. We also came up with a list of questions that needed further exploration with those two candidates. The head of HR and I would take on this final interview.

In this way, the selection funnel narrows and we ask some specific questions and record their answers in their personnel file. We keep their responses so we can review these with them in the future to see how we're doing.

In this final interview we made sure to expose all the "warts" of the job, so that they knew exactly what they were getting into. We gave these candidates plenty of opportunity to ask us about the job and the organization. We saw it as a red flag if someone hadn't prepared any questions for us.

This process is very important in building trust with the potential employee and maintaining that trust if we hire them. We call this the PAT process (Performance, Attainment and Trust).

We used our values to generate many of our interview questions. For example, one of our values stated: "I will do the right thing with integrity by being honest with myself and respecting others and being transparent, saying what I mean and meaning what I say." We would ask candidates to give us specific examples of how they have demonstrated this value:

- Please give me a couple of examples of when you've had to be honest with yourself.
- Tell me about a time when you treated someone with respect in the workplace.
- Please give me an example of how you treated someone with respect in your personal life.

※ Think of a time when you disrespected someone. Please explain. (Push for examples.)

※ We also asked questions like: Can you please describe for me your career goals? Where do you see your career leading you?

※ We ask this question to determine whether their career goals align with those of our organization.

※ Also, if their goals do align with ours, are we in a position to help them reach their goals?

※ This question also provides clarity on what they expect and how soon.

※ This tells you what they aspire to become.

※ Will this person be an "eagle" or an "owl"? (We'll explain these terms below.)

SELECTION

We also conducted all the necessary reference checks—both those the candidate provided as well as those they didn't provide.

Finally, in our senior management meeting we discussed the one or two remaining candidates ensuring that the whole team had input on the decision. We wanted each of the leaders to have a stake in these hiring decisions. In this way, we were all more apt to develop the new employee. None of us would be able to complain later that we had not had input into the hiring of this employee.

All along the selection process, the organization owes it to the candidates to communicate clearly about the process, what's expected at each phase and where the candidate stands. Organizations typically fail miserably at this, leaving candidates feeling cheated and disrespected. Such an organization is inadvertently communicating by their actions that this is "just a job" and the candidate is "just a number."

In contrast to that we want to cast vision for the candidate about the mission of our organization in such a way that they desperately want to work for us and will work hard to stay there. We also want to look at the candidate's goals and see how theirs and ours overlap. Can we mutually benefit one another?

In general, here are some of the things we were looking for in a candidate:

- Honest
- Energetic
- Enthusiastic
- Sense of humor
- Passion for work
- Genuine and truthful
- Intellectual curiosity
- Handles stress well
- Executes effectively
- Strong personal values

- Likeable
- Humble
- Catalyzer
- Decisive
- Solid knowledge
- Communicates well
- Cares about others
- Takes responsibility
- Pushes through obstacles
- Engages others

- Confident
- Optimistic
- Proactive
- Loves to learn
- Embraces change
- Constructively competitive
- Sets realistic goals
- Good under pressure
- Works well on their own
- Pursues results

One thing to keep in mind about the selection process is not to allow yourself to be seduced by job experience. Early in my career I placed too much emphasis on a person's experience and not enough on values. This is easy to do in a crisis when you feel that you must fill an important role quickly.

Step back and be patient. Make sure that the candidate aligns with your values. Your patience will be handsomely rewarded down the road instead of having to fill this position again in a year because you didn't do the work you should have done in the first place.

INITIATING EMPLOYEE DEVELOPMENT

Once we hired an employee I asked additional questions to get to know them and begin to develop a plan for them. By having this session with the employee early on it accelerated building a relationship of trust.

Please describe what you expect to attain while in this position? What do you want to achieve in the next two-to-three years?

- This grants you more clarity on their expectations.
- Can this position deliver on their expectations?
- Take the opportunity to coach them in terms of their knowledge and experience and the time it generally takes to achieve what they desire.

What do you think you need to learn in order to achieve those goals?

- This is important information that you can put in their personal development plan.
- By beginning to create a personal development plan now, you are gaining their trust and demonstrating your concern for their development.

﹩ Ensure they understand that their development is something they are responsible for, not you. But you can open doors for them and provide an environment in which they can grow.

What other work experience and/or skills will you require to achieve those goals?

﹩ This information again goes in their personal development plan.

﹩ This may also provide information regarding their training needs.

What are your personal goals?

﹩ We may like to think we can separate work from home life, but people are integrated beings. Their personal goals will ultimately affect their work.

﹩ What is most important to them? Can our organization and this position help them achieve that?

﹩ Knowing their personal goals also helps us customize future rewards when they achieve extraordinary results.

How often would you like to meet to review your progress?

﹩ Some employees like a lot of feedback, while others prefer very little. (I had a basic standard of delivering feedback and maintained a high level of contact with them.)

﹩ We explain our corporate standard of one annual review with ongoing communication regarding expectations and performance throughout the year.

***Please tell me what you understand you will be account-
able for in this position.***

- Make sure they understand the position and its
  responsibilities.

- Clarify anything they are foggy on.

How will you describe great performance in this position?

- How well does their concept of "great performance"
  match up with yours?

- Stretch them if necessary and make it clear what great
  performance means to you.

- If the candidate expresses low performance this should
  be a red flag and needs to be addressed immediately!

- If you measure it and reward it, people will excel at it
  (the Hawthorne Effect).

What other questions do you have?

- This question communicates not only its intent, but the
  subtlety that communication goes both ways in our organization. We value them and their input as employees.

Discussion Questions

1. Discuss why true competitive advantage comes from its people.

2. The author described The Leadership Code with the analogy of a bicycle wheel with the organization's values represented by the hub and its employees by its spokes. Describe a situation in which you have experienced either a serious "wobble" in your organization due to a faulty "spoke", or smooth, efficient traction in the organization because everyone was functioning at their best in the right roles within your organization.

3. In the recruiting and hiring phase, why do you think we generally focus too intently on skill-set and not enough on values?

4. Discuss the statement: "Your selection process should radiate your organization's values."

5. In what ways, can you as an organization's leader be involved in the training and development of your employees?

CHAPTER SIX

People First: Employee Assessment

*You measure your people
and you take action on those that don't measure up.*
– Jack Welch

Employee assessment is a key element in a "people-first" approach to leadership. Employees genuinely want to know where the organization is going and how they can contribute to its success. They desperately desire clarity around what is expected of them and they need the tools and environment in which they can excel.

What I'm describing reinforces the fact that we must invert the pyramid in terms of our leadership. Today's new CEO is the Chief Employee Officer. That means that he or she is at the bottom and the frontline employees are at the top.

The frontline employees are the ones interfacing directly with the customers. For this reason, we need to equip them to make as many of the day-to-day decisions as possible. Let me share a couple of examples that demonstrate the need for employees to be empowered to make these kinds of decisions.

When we first moved to Cyprus to set up the new contact center, we were terribly hindered by the old bureaucracy of the parent organization in Toronto. Back in Canada, the finance department was given the authority to be the gatekeeper of every penny we spent in Cyprus. Our financial transactions numbered soon in the thousands, yet the home office had a process in place that required their stamp of approval on every refund or expense over $25.

Without the authority to process these on our own, we were hamstrung and could not conduct business in an efficient or professional manner. As soon as possible, we changed the process so we could make the necessary decisions in Cyprus. This took a lot of lobbying and fact-based support to change, because of how entrenched the old-school thinking was.

Many leaders make the mistake of thinking they have to hold on to these small decisions. If they do, it will not only be to *their* ruin, but also to the detriment of the organization, its customers and its employees. Many times leaders ask, "Why change? It's always been this way." And individuals and organizations typically will not change unless there is a crisis.

The contact center provides another clear example for the need to push the day-to-day decisions to the first-line employees. One of our chief performance measures focused on *first contact resolution*. In other words, if a customer service representative (CSR) could resolve a customer's issue in that initial contact, we had happier customers and saved ourselves time and money.

Our first contact resolution goal was 90 percent. Obviously, the employees had to be well-trained, authorized and empowered to make the kinds of decisions we wanted them to make.

And we had to reward them for making those decisions and ensure that we didn't inadvertently punish them when their decision went awry.

Initially, our first contact resolution (FCR) numbers were extremely low. We carefully tracked them and our quality team reviewed calls and assessed what needed to change. Then we shared that information with our trainers who designed training and development experiences to better equip our customer service reps.

Early on, we realized that one reason our FCR numbers were so low was because the little decisions we needed to be able to make still resided with someone else in Toronto. We had to re-write policies and decision-making processes in order to give the front-line employees authority to make these decisions. This required a lot of re-engineering of the decision-making process. Then we gave the employees more training and continued to measure, watching the FCR numbers go up.

We kept measuring, assessing, training and measuring again. Everyone knew exactly how they were doing and we continually stretched to the next goal. Eventually, we consistently achieved world-class first contact resolution metrics of over 90 percent. This process can be applied to every business and is not just confined to the contact center business.

Pushing the day-to-day decisions to the first-line employees requires more than measuring and training however. The time you've spent building trust with your employees is vital to the success of the inverted pyramid. Employees have to know that they can take the "risk" of making a financial decision on behalf of the company without fear of reprimand or losing their job.

Additionally, you must define the boundaries within which employees can make decisions. We also want to broaden those boundaries, freeing up the front-line employees to make as many decisions as possible. This gives the employees a strong sense of trust and empowerment. They feel important, because they are!

If we remove the doing and deciding away from a job, we take the fun out of the job as well. Autonomy brings passion and engagement. Your employees become "vested partners" in the business.

Well-hired employees with strong values will not abuse this freedom, but will strive to please you, serve the customer well, and benefit the organization. Naturally, you'll always have a few employees who will push the boundaries to see what happens. This is why a values-based approach is so important. Leading by values will help weed out those employees who do abuse their freedom.

Along these lines, you must be tough when a serious value is broken. I stated earlier that a full half of performance evaluation rests on the values. If an employee cannot hold to the values, we must let them go decisively and quickly. This demonstrates to the organization that behaviors contrary to our values are not acceptable.

Once, we had two employees who were very likable. In fact, one of these employees was a star performer. He was a quick learner, smart and was moving up in the organization. But he had one character flaw that surfaced—he would often show up late to work. So, we put him on a performance plan for his tardiness. His character flaw raised a red flag. When you see these things, they usually lead to bigger things down the road.

Sometime later, this employee gambled with virtual money that we used to test our products. Our virtual bank accounts cost us real money. He and another employee skimmed funds they had access to and used them for their own personal use. Their blatant breach of integrity cost them their jobs.

There is a principle at work here that states, "One who is faithful in little will be faithful in much." And the negative of that principle holds true as well that the person who is negligent in little will be negligent in much. For this reason, any violation of a core value—no matter how slight—is a red flag and must be dealt with.

This story also demonstrates the fallacy of focusing solely on performance to the exclusion of adherence to values. If a person is struggling with performance, we will patiently work with them over time. But if a person is struggling with holding to our values, the performance improvement plan for that person will be very short.

VALUES-PERFORMANCE MATRIX

Although we have not discussed the formulation of your organization's values in detail, we have made it clear that the organization must be values-based. In terms of employees at every level of the organization, we recruit, hire, train, measure and reward based on these core values. We have also stated that a full 50 percent of an employee's performance evaluation must focus on adherence to the values.

When we are selecting employees for any position—whether your senior management team, or front-line employee—we do so on the basis of how well their values align with ours. Performance is the second measure we use after values. This also holds true in terms of the performance review process.

The following Values-Performance Matrix (VPM) Assessment Tool illustrates what this practice looks like graphically portrayed.

VPM Assessment Tool

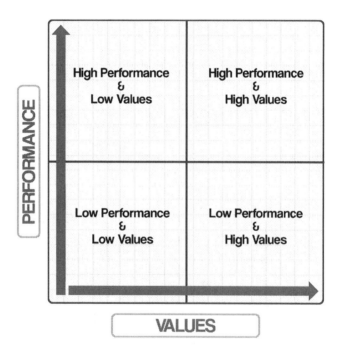

Let's look at this VPM Assessment Tool in greater detail:

The bottom left quadrant—low values and low performance

※ Anyone who falls in this quadrant is a cancer to you and the organization.

※ These people do not perform, they blame their poor performance on everyone else, they are a constant distraction, and they never seem to be doing anything. They're always on a break.

※ These people only inhibit any initiative you want to take.

※ These employees consume your time and are your greatest frustrations.

※ Eliminate this person from the organization as soon as possible.

The top right quadrant—high performance and high values

※ These employees are your "A" players.

※ They lead with values and have the performance to back it up.

※ They are well-respected in the organization and everyone wants them on their team. If they are in leadership, people love working for them.

※ These are the people you want working for you. They will propel your organization forward and bring others up with them. Seek to build your organization around these people. They are your foundation, so entrust them with much!

The top left quadrant—high performance and low values

※ This quadrant is the most controversial of the four quadrants.

※ Most organizations see this person as the "Rock Star"— the person who consistently hits a home run.

※ This employee is often among the highest paid employees and always maxes out on their bonus.

- Ironically, most people can't stand this employee and wish you would fire them.

- Senior management often believes they could not survive without this person and this person openly throws it in their face.

- A person in this quadrant leverages their high performance to get their way and will step on anyone who gets in their way.

- This person generally has a huge ego and regularly puts people down in front of everyone in meetings and group settings.

- They are always talking behind other's backs.

- They are not a team player and they break all the rules, feeling that the rules don't apply to them.

- They make up their own rules as they go to ensure their success.

- You can never really trust what they are telling you.

- You need to read this person the riot act and present to them your values and how you expect them to behave.

- You must have the shortest leash on this person and the least amount of patience. We do not allow breeches of values—period.

- Communicate to them that the team comes first.

- Put them on a values performance plan for 3 to 6 months with weekly and monthly meetings to evaluate and document progress.

- Here's what you can expect based on my experience:
  - Although some values can be learned, many of them come from one's upbringing.

- A person without values cannot see why they are even necessary.

- Ego blinds such a person to the necessity for change.

- Although very few change (some never had anyone challenge them before), both you and the employee will see after the first month which way things are going and whether it will be best for the employee to leave.

- You can offer a graceful exit (which usually appeals to their ego) and work out the details to get them out of the organization.

- Such a decision to let your star player go for failure to align with the organization's values is huge. This will create ripples throughout the organization that you are serious about values. This one act can profoundly change your organization.

The bottom right quadrant—low performance and high values

- This quadrant is also misunderstood by many organizations, because they put performance over values. I'm advocating that we reverse our mindsets 180 degrees in this regard. High Values will lead an organization to high performance and not the other way around.

- Organizations tend to have less patience for these people and fire them more readily than those in the top left quadrant, but the likelihood of a turnaround is much greater with them.

- An employee in this quadrant is producing average to below average results.

- Everyone generally likes this person.

⚌ They are a team player, always supporting their peers and their employees.

⚌ This person always has something good to say about everyone and never backbites anyone.

⚌ They always seem to be working, but their results are mediocre at best.

⚌ They are receptive to any new initiative and always want to be a part of it.

⚌ Here's what you can expect based on my experience:

- Because you have made values the priority of your organization, these are people you want to develop and retain.

- Be more patient with these people by putting them on a longer probationary period: six to nine months if you are seeing improvement. We gave them a little more rope, but they were underachieving and performance is vital. We did not retain employees who could not perform well.

- Communicate clearly with them that you appreciate their values, but in the end they need to deliver results and they are behind expectations.

- Ask them why they think they are falling short. You may be surprised what you learn. They may be in the wrong job, they may not know exactly what is expected of them, they may lack a skill like time management or planning and organization, etc.

- Be quick to offer training and support to get them on track.

- Set clear goals and expectations with the employee. Put them on a performance plan and let them give you the targets and timelines in which they will achieve them. Because these employees are high in values, they want to over-deliver, so make sure their goals are not too aggressive for them to achieve.

- By following this plan, if you eventually have to let them go, you have made your job easier because they understand and respect your reasons. They were unable to meet the goals and standards that they set for themselves. In this case, allow them to leave gracefully and assist them any way you can in their transition. These are good people, but their skill set was not a good fit for your organization.

THE ABCS OF PERFORMANCE

Similar to Jack Welch with General Electric and others, we adopted a system to identify levels of employee performance. People either performed at an A, B, or C level.[6]

- A = Top performer, high values. Level A performance indicates that this person consistently over-delivers. Typically, an organization may start with 20% of its workforce ranking as an "A".

- B = Above average values and performance. These are good, solid employees. They are good at what they do, but not promotable. The organization needs these performers. Perhaps 50% of the workforce falls in this category.

- C = Average or below in values and performance. These people we put on a performance plan for improvement. If they couldn't improve, we let them go. Initially, they comprised about 30% of our organization. Every year we endeavored to "call out" the C's to either help them improve or purge them from the organization.

We also discovered that once a manager had been leading a team for three years, he/she became blind to the C's on their team. So from time to time we would swap out managers on a team. The new manager would come in and expose the C's. We called this "muscle-building", or constantly upgrading the team.

Because of this ever-present focus on improving our teams, we instituted an aggressive succession planning process. If we moved an A up, we knew exactly who we had in line to replace them. This was all part of our performance review process. (I'll describe this process in detail in chapter 8.)

Through our performance review process, every employee knew exactly where they stood: A, B, or C employee. We also made it clear to them what "A" performance looked like and how they could attain it. Eventually, we moved to the place where we had nearly all A and B employees. Any C's we put on a performance plan or let go.

Let me mention a principle here: Don't confuse *rocking the boat* with poor performance. We had an "A" employee named Olga. She was an outstanding employee as a Customer Service Representative, so we promoted her to the position of Shift Supervisor. But when performance reviews came around, she was really tough on her employees—to the extent that some were in tears.

Olga's boss assumed that she couldn't manage others well and wanted to let her go. ("Why else would they be crying?") I always got personally involved with the situation when we talked about letting someone go. I believe in the principle of always maintaining a good relationship with your manager's boss. In this case, I was the boss.

When we looked into Olga's behavior, what we discovered was that she was the only shift supervisor who was actually carrying out the performance reviews like we wanted. Her behavior was "rocking the boat" because she outperformed all the other shift supervisors. Her employees had never been held to this high standard, that's why they were upset.

We also discovered that a C-level manager will get rid of their "A" employees. In this particular case, we found fault with Olga's boss, not with her, so we let him go. Her boss wanted to fire her because he didn't want to be upstaged or held accountable to the higher standard by which she was working. In this way, "A" employees represent a threat to "C" managers, so the "C" manager will try to get rid of them. As you'll see in the next chapter, our performance review system seeks to expose problems like this quickly.

EAGLES, OWLS, SEAGULLS AND TURKEYS

More recently, I developed a helpful method for categorizing employees. I've found that employees generally fell into one of four groups: eagles, owls, seagulls and turkeys.

Eagles – True to their name, these people soar! These are your "A" employees. Eagles continually and consistently over-deliver. They require very little maintenance. They are proactive and take challenges head-on. Some eagles are specialists, but deliver spectacular results. Others may not blow you away with spectacular results, but with the volume of things they can accomplish.

Some eagles have limited people skills and for some it's their greatest strength. As managers, their ability to motivate others and get people to do extraordinary things is amazing. They are able to instill trust immediately in those they meet.

Other eagles have raw brain power and know how to learn quickly, grasp difficult concepts fast and put them to work. Eagles are extremely loyal.

No one person who worked for me had all of the above qualities, nor do I. Instead, they're like the X-Men—each one has something that they're extremely good at, which more than compensated for any weaknesses they may have had. Eagles always exceeded expectations.

Owls – These people are wise and immovable. Owls are usually your rock-solid, long-term employees. Owls could be "A" or "B" employees. Owls may have been eagles at one time, but life, marriage and children have taken priority in their lives, so that *stability* has become their motivation.

Owls are people who just want to stay in one place and be the best they can be in one specific role. And we need people like that. You can count on them. They share their wisdom up and down through the organization liberally. Owls often serve as mentors for eagles.

In a managerial role, owls have no problem hiring people smarter than they are. Owls are typically some of your best role models for your values. Be careful not to overlook owls or fail to celebrate them.

Another caution with owls: if they become "B's" in the organization, their longevity may be at risk. You can only have so many "B's" in a job, discipline or managing role, or they may become a bottleneck for the advancement of the "A's". We need runway for the "A's". So we need to let "B" owls know where they stand and urge them to improve and excel.

Seagulls – These folks squawk about everything and crap on everyone! Seagulls are your poorest performing employees. They are the "C's" in your organization. Errors are never their fault. Their value set is inconsistent. They hide from taking responsibility and making decisions.

Seagulls try to befriend others by telling them whatever they want to hear. If a seagull is a manager, their team is usually full of under-performing, weak employees. ("Birds of a feather flock together.") If they perceive that someone on their team threatens their leadership, they try to get rid of them. They never hire anyone smarter than they are.

Seagulls constantly talk behind others' backs and always want to engage in the latest gossip. They take credit for the work their team does. They don't promote others and are jealous when someone else gets the promotion.

Sometimes a person is identified as a seagull, but they are just in the wrong job or they have a seagull boss who doesn't know how to manage or motivate them.

Turkeys – These employees were eagles or owls who have reached their maximum development and the organization has moved beyond them. It could be that they were promoted too quickly, or they just don't have the talent or "runway" to be stretched any further.

Turkeys are now failing in their role. All of their previous equity begins to deteriorate and they fall from grace. People see them as "turkeys ready for slaughter" (ready to be fired). Others say of them, "He/she used to be so good, what happened?"

When you recognize a turkey, step in and try to get them back into an owl's role in which they can consistently live the values and deliver at a high level again. They'll be happier too!

Hopefully in this chapter I've convinced you of the importance of both values and performance and that while performance can be trained, values often cannot be trained. Metrics and reporting are other key elements of the performance review process. We'll cover those and related topics in the following chapters.

Discussion Questions

1. Discuss the concept of the inverted pyramid and why the CEO of an organization today must serve as the Chief Employee Officer.

2. Why do many managers think they have to hold onto all the decision-making in their organization? In what ways does this backfire on them?

3. Explain why values alignment must take precedence over performance from a priority focus standpoint.

4. Consider the Values-Performance Matrix Assessment Tool. Which quadrant of employees have you struggled with most? Why do you think this is?

5. What additional recommendations would you make for addressing an employee who is in the upper-left quadrant—high performance, low values?

6. How would you deal with the employee who is in the lower-right quadrant of low performance and high values?

CHAPTER SEVEN

People First: Performance Management

You can expect what you inspect.
– W. Edwards Deming

In a nutshell, leading people in business involves:

- Hiring the right people for the right positions
- Providing clear expectations
- Training and equipping them with the right tools
- Providing regular feedback on how they're doing
- Making it your mission to support them

In chapter four, we looked at the tendency for leaders to lean toward two extremes: direct leadership and consensus leadership. We noted that while there's a place for both styles, neither style can serve us as a failsafe fallback style. And of course, there are other leadership styles as well.

Similarly, we've also emphasized a people-first mindset that gives weight to both values and performance. In this regard too, we must doggedly avoid swinging the pendulum to one extreme or the other. A people-first orientation does not mean that we don't measure performance or hold people to specific standards. On the contrary, performance management is a key element in a people-first approach to leadership. There is no conflict between operating a business *for* peak performance and *with* a people-first focus.

In this chapter, we'll direct our attention toward the metrics and reporting elements of performance management.

The Hawthorne Effect

The Hawthorne Effect came about as the result of a study conducted around 1930. What we take away from The Hawthorne Effect is that employee performance will improve if we pay attention to it (i.e, *measure* it); and employee performance will improve exponentially if we *measure* it and *report* it.

For this reason, measurement and reporting are the two pillars of performance management.

MEASURING PERFORMANCE

Performance management requires that we *measure* performance. Metrics flow out of our vision and mission. Our metrics are an attempt to craft clear, measurable goals around what our vision aspires to accomplish.

We used the graphic on the following page to reinforce with employees the importance of tracking metrics.

You can't tell if you are winning if you don't keep score!

Meaningful metrics measure not only *what* we will do but *how* we will do it. The *how* has its roots in our values. Here again, there should be no conflict or confusion between metrics and values. If we think we have to sacrifice our values to reach our metrics, then we have the wrong metrics. Our values should always assist us in *reaching* our goals not *deterring* us from them.

Additionally, there will always be some metrics that are common throughout the organization, coming from the senior management team. But as you drill down in the organization, the departments will have other metrics they need to focus on. The key is that these other metrics always must support one of the major key topline metrics.

Besides referring to our values, vision and mission, we can look to other sources to help establish our metrics. Some of these other sources include:

- Internal requirements from shareholders such as financial performance
- Competitors' goals and metrics—are they measuring things we don't measure, but should?
- Other industries with similar metrics that can help us benchmark world-class performance

Metrics are our *goals.* These are represented by a specific number or measure of some kind. We establish overall organizational goals, goals for each department or work group, and goals for each employee. All subordinate goals must serve the overarching goals of the organization. We also create long-term metrics or goals three or five years out and then break those down into bite-size pieces.

The Strategic Waterfall graphic below illustrates the relationship between these elements:

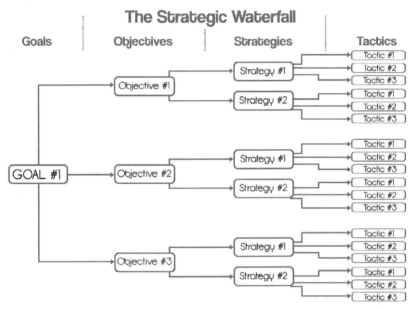

% *Objectives* define *what* we will do to achieve the goals.

% *Strategies* describe *how* we will attain the goals and objectives.

% *Tactics* specifically describe the *who, where* and *when* of reaching our goals and objectives.

It's also important that we communicate clearly to employees *why* a particular goal is important. For instance, we can blow the horn all day long about employee retention. But until managers understand how employee retention can be a huge drain on resources and profoundly impact the bottom line, there's no impetus to improve. But note the impact of a simple graphic targeting this issue:

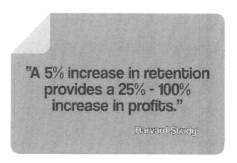

"A 5% increase in retention provides a 25% - 100% increase in profits."

Harvard Study

A reason like that will get a manager's attention, especially if their evaluation and compensation depends on it!

Along these lines, make sure that you're tracking both *leading* and *lagging* metrics. Lagging metrics are important, grand measures that tell us after-the-fact how we performed. In a given month, we might have reported that our turnover rate was 45 percent, or that our first contact resolution rate was 60 percent. Those are *lagging* indicators, meaning that we can never go back and change those months. We cannot manage what is past, but those numbers do give us a scorecard of how we're doing against our stated goals. Lagging indicators are also helpful in tracking long-term progress.

Leading indicators are those elements of our metrics that tell us what we have to measure along the way to ensure that we attain a 5 percent turnover rate or 90 percent first contact resolution. Leading indicators are *process metrics*. We can and must measure these all along the way, at every stage of a process. It's the "measure twice, cut once" principle of the woodworker.

By measuring leading indicators, we know that each employee is performing in a way that we have determined will ensure success. This is where Deming's mantra comes into play, "You can expect what you inspect." For instance, one of our leading indicators (metrics) for our CSRs was that they follow the script exactly. Doing so guaranteed success.

Managing and motivating your employees is the driver for your success. You need to get them to believe they can deliver extraordinary results. This requires that you track and keep them accountable for their responsibilities and commitments. We review a manager's performance based on how well they are at muscle-building their team and keeping their employees on track with their goals.

The greater danger for most of us is not aiming too high and not reaching our target, but aiming too low and hitting it.
– Michelangelo

Following is a chart showing a snapshot of our top ten organizational metrics measured against world class performance.

Benchmark Against World Class Key Performance Indicators:

Top 10 KPI's	World Class Targets	Actual
Answer Emails	90% / 1 HR	98%
Answer Calls	80% / 20 Sec	96%
Quality - Emails/Calls	95%	98%
Call Abandon Rate (English Only)	< 2%	2%
First Contact Resolution	90%	92%
Number of Interactions per Active Player	10%	10%
Employee Satisfaction	90%	91%
Customer Satisfaction	90%	90%
Employee Turnover	10%	8%
Annual Cost Savings	3%	4%

People need goals and milestones to focus on and rally around. People want to know what's expected of them and they love a challenge. They thrive on attaining measurable goals, keeping score and tracking their improvement. There's no better morale-booster than tracking and seeing continuous growth and improvement over time. But we have to establish metrics and measure frequently in order for that to function. This is where reporting comes in.

REPORTING

I'm a firm believer in reporting metrics as frequently and graphically as possible. Measuring performance and not reporting it or hiding the results is as bad as not measuring at all—possibly worse. But first, we need to get the message across that we have a problem before we develop the metrics to solve it. And sometimes a graphic representation is the best way to get that message across.

At one point, we were struggling with customer retention. We designed the following "leaky bucket" visual to portray what was happening. We were working so hard acquiring new customers, but because of other system failures, we were losing them as fast as we acquired them! This graphic helped us figure out how to "plug" existing holes and keep new ones from occurring. And by doing so, we could spend a whole lot less time acquiring new customers.

"The bigger the leak in our bucket of customers the harder we have to work to fill it up and keep it full."

Once we agreed on the World Class performance target and the time it would take to get there, we would plot the target and the actual performance as we went along. I am a firm believer in the power of the subconscious mind and visualization. If the goal was over a longer period of time we asked the person responsible to provide monthly targets to achieve that would ultimately help us reach our goal. We plotted these targets and the overall goal and measured the actual against them.

Below is such a Performance Management type chart reporting actual performance against world class performance.

Quality

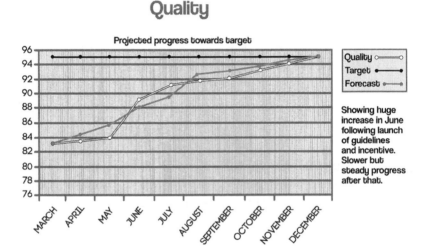

If it's important that employees know results daily, then figure out a way to report them daily. On other measures, perhaps weekly or monthly is sufficient. But keep in mind, the closer to the event that metrics are reported, the more likely they will improve. We have no power to change what happened a month ago.

If frontline employees have a direct impact on the organization's bottom line, as in the case with our contact center representatives, then we would track their metrics, publish the results, and pay the top performers accordingly.

We published these metrics monthly, sent them to everyone and put the results on the community board. We calculated the average and one, two and three standard deviations above and below that average.

We used a color-coded system in which gold was reserved for star performance. Then we adopted the traffic light colors for the remaining performance levels: green—on the mark; yellow—warning; and red—needing a performance plan. We gave bonuses to the top reps (gold performers). Nobody received a bonus for average or below average performance.

Reps that performed at one or more standard deviations below average we sent for training to help them improve. If after training their results did not improve, we put them on a performance improvement plan. We gave new reps a six-month probationary period to perform at expected levels. This system created a friendly competition that continuously raised the bar as new reps would win each month achieving higher and higher scores.

On the next page is a more sophisticated example of how we tracked individual employee performance. In this graph, the gold employees received a bonus check at the end of the month and the red employees were put on a performance plan. Notice in the example below that 80 percent performance was unacceptable given our lofty goal.

Customer Service Performance

CONTACT CENTER OVERALL SCORE

Sometimes new employees coming out of training we identified as "rockets" because they surpassed veterans after only a few months. We paid the bonuses by physical check each month rather than merely adding it to their paycheck. This reinforced the fact that this was a reward for superior performance. Also, by paying bonuses monthly we created a much closer link between performance and reward.

In terms of rewards, plaques and other types of recognition are good, but money is king. Don't let good people leave for lack of recognition or money.

You can also use training and personal development as a key motivator. For example, during my career, Jack Welch was my inspiration. My boss back then, Lewis, knew this. One time he suggested I go to Boston to participate in a three-day conference that Jack was hosting. This was a huge motivator for me and demonstrated how much my manager cared about me and my development in the organization. (Lewis was an accountant by profession, so he was very careful with money, which added to the impact of his gesture.)

What I've been describing in this chapter is the heart and soul of this book! The business world hasn't focused enough on how to implement measurement and reporting day-to-day. In the following chapter, we'll show you a specific, time-tested process for measuring and reporting value-based performance.

Discussion Questions

1. What is the link between values and performance when establishing your metrics?

2. List some of the metrics that apply to your whole organization. What are some examples of metrics that apply more specifically to one department?

3. Explain the difference between leading and lagging metrics. What are some examples of leading metrics that you consistently track in your organization?

4. What are some of the ways that you currently report on your performance metrics in your organization? What additional ways for reporting performance would you like to implement?

5. A graphic portrayal can be very effective in reporting performance. In what ways does your organization graphically illustrate performance measures? In what ways could you improve on this?

CHAPTER EIGHT

The VPA-DS Process

We pay for results, not effort.
– Michael McCain

We can measure this-and-that all day long and even report it all, but unless we hold individual employees accountable for their performance, the measuring and reporting hold no power for improvement. Also, it's not how hard you work, but how you perform. Are you getting results?

Do not do what a manager did to me once. In December of that year he invited me out for coffee. When I sat down at the table, he pulled out a napkin and began jotting down a few things pertaining to my performance: good and bad—all examples from the past four weeks. That napkin was the extent of my "performance review" that year!

I was utterly frustrated and didn't trust this manager's process at all. As a result, in the future I committed to provide my employees a robust, thoughtful, effective process for reviewing their performance.

THE VPA-DS MODEL

Below is a graphic that shows the process we developed for measuring and reporting performance. We call it the Values, Performance and Assessment—Development and Succession Planning process or the VPA-DS. As you can see it involves seven critical elements within the performance evaluation process:

1. Setting expectations

2. Collecting performance data

3. Initiating the annual performance review process by the employee

4. The employee's manager assesses the employee's performance

5. Management then meets to force-rank employees, thereby creating a career path and succession plan

6. Conducting feedback discussions with employees

7. Implementing actions—training and development and performance actions

Note that each critical element is either on-going or has a specific time line associated with it. Also—and this is very important—each critical element is followed (and preceded) by coaching from the employee's manager. Continuous coaching is a core element of a people-first approach to leading others.

This coaching piece is so critical because it ensures that the employee always knows exactly what's expected of them by when and to what degree. There are no surprises, no withholding of information, and this demonstrates that the manager is there to help the employee succeed. We want them to succeed, because their performance impacts the bottom line.

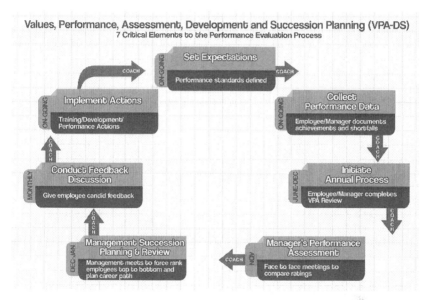

Values, Performance, Assessment, Development and Succession Planning (VPA-DS)
7 Critical Elements to the Performance Evaluation Process

You can access a pdf of The Values-Performance-Assessment (VPA) form that we used by going to this link: *www. UnlockLeadershipCode.com/VPADS*. The VPA-DS has two primary sections:

1. **The values section** was worth 50% of their evaluation and deals with their behaviors as they reflect company values.

2. **The performance section** was 40%, with another 10% granted for completing the development plan. The 10% was given to ensure that employees took their development seriously and knew that we were investing in them.

HOW TO ADMINISTER THE VPA-DS MODEL

As the VPA-DS graphic makes clear, the VPA is just one element in the annual employee assessment process. We should be gathering information, compiling supporting examples of good and bad behavior all year long.

1. Managers, be prepared to spend a significant amount of time writing your reviews. Support each line in the review with evidence gathered throughout the year. True, many of the examples will be more recent because employees should be improving. You don't want to mark someone down for an issue that happened much earlier in the year and that has completely been dealt with and changed. We usually allowed 4-6 weeks for the managers to complete the VPA-DS.

2. Ensure that you give the employee plenty of time to complete the VPA-DS in advance of their review. They are responsible to complete a copy of the VPA-DS, evaluating and scoring themselves in each section. They too must supply supporting evidence. We gave the employees 4 weeks to complete the VPA-DS on themselves.

3. Both the manager and individual employees meet to go over the VPA-DS. This involves first comparing the ratings of both the manager and the employee. This process is extremely powerful for orientating an employee's perception of their performance with your perception of their performance.

    This comparison is critically important to building trust in your relationship with that employee. When you disagree with their assessment, it's vital that you have done your homework to support your assessment with examples. Calibrating employee-employer assessment is critical for trust and driving employee motivation.

Below is an abbreviated graphic of the Values Performance Assessment form. You can access a full version of the VPA-DS form online. In the working, online version there are three tabs at the bottom of the spreadsheet. A tab each for: values, competency (performance), and general. The general tab addressed things like: assessing the employee's career; a place for employee, manager, and the two-up manager's comments; signatures, and an overall summary assessment.

Performance Assessment Form

Employee's Name:		Job Title:	
Department:		Date in Position:	
Period Covered by Assessment:		Manager's Name:	

	Role Model	Potential Leader	Progressing	Needs Improvement
Values	One of our most effective leaders demonstrating this capability factor in the role. A Role Model, someone who could coach others in this factor.	Someone who understands this factor and is able to demonstrate this capability efficiently in the role.	Someone who understands this factor but would benefit from developmental Coaching and work assignments designed to increase their level of capability in the role.	Someone who does not yet understand this factor. Is not able to demonstrate it effectively. Would benefit from Direction to better understand and needs development assignments.

A. Do the right thing with integrity - by	Employee	Manager	Employee	Manager	Employee	Manager	Employee	Manager
A1 - Being Honest to ourselves and respecting others, always Fair								
A2 - Being transparent, Open and Trusting of each other								

Place an "X" in the appropriate section

| Employee's Comments/Examples: | | Manager's Comments/Examples: | |

B. Perform - by	Employee	Manager	Employee	Manager	Employee	Manager	Employee	Manager
B1 - Having the passion to be the best								
B2 - Setting stretch targets and rewarding results								
B3 - Taking ownership and being accountable for actions/results								

Place an "X" in the appropriate section

The print on the graphic of the Values Performance Assessment form above is small, so let me provide for you here the four *ratings* and their explanation:

1. **Role Model** – One of our most effective leaders demonstrating this capability factor in the role. A Role Model, someone who could coach others in this factor.

2. **Potential Leader** – Someone who understands this factor and is able to demonstrate this capability efficiently in the role.

3. **Progressing** – Someone who understands this factor but would benefit from developmental Coaching and work assignments designed to increase their level of capability in the role.

4. **Needs Improvement** – Someone who does not yet understand this factor. Is not able to demonstrate it effectively. Would benefit from Direction to better understand and needs development assignments.

In your first time conducting a VPA-DS with your organization, start the process with your senior management and work down through the organization. By doing so, you will model how the process works, how to deal with special situations, and demonstrate your buy-in. In this way your managers become comfortable with the process and can better teach the process to their direct reports.

Let's consider a couple scenarios that may ensue during the performance review with the employee.

Tied performance evaluation scores

In this scenario, both the manager and the employee rated the employee the same. This can happen often, especially when you've had previous performance discussions with the employee. With time, the employee is calibrated to and aligned with what is expected.

1. *Make sure you agree on the scores for the same reasons.*
   This is particularly important if this is the first time using

the VPA-DS. I always liked to let the employee go first. I had to make sure I carefully listened and that I understood what they were saying. I wanted to communicate that I really cared and needed their commitment. There must be open discussion around the rationale and evidence to ensure that both parties agree with the scores.

2. *Seek agreement based on evidence and make any adjustments to the scores.* The top score must be a stretch—difficult to reach. Not everyone can attain it. Hand it out judiciously and only to those top people who are clearly the recognized best on that measure. This also teaches your employees that you have very high expectations and if they don't receive a top score then it is your job to clearly articulate what a top score looks like and what that employee needs to do to achieve it.

   We worked very hard to provide examples of what a top score looked like by linking it to a person, or another clear example of "A" behavior. You could not go through the review without clearly articulating what the top box or "A" performance looked like.

   When you first launch the VPA-DS system, some people will be shocked and disappointed at how low some of their scores are. But you need to explain to them that the system is new and now that they know what the organization expects from them you have confidence that this will improve tremendously. For high achievers this may be a first for them because they have always been a top performer and have never experienced a low mark in anything. A low mark does not mean they are a bad person, it just means that they aren't used to living and leading the values outwardly.

You mark the employee higher than they mark themselves

This is always a pleasant situation to be in and it brings a smile to the employee's face and bolsters their confidence. It's important to go through the same process described above. You need to understand their reasoning and support yours with evidence.

In a case like this, I would consider adjusting my scores down, but never all the way to the level at which the employee rated themselves. There may be situations or factors that I had overlooked. Also, some people are naturally hard on themselves. The performance review process helps us calibrate the employee to our measures.

Your score is lower than their score

This situation is more likely to occur when you first institute the VPA-DS process because prior to this there was little calibration of values and performance expectations and processes. We follow the same protocol as above, but this scenario usually takes the longest because we must talk everything out and ensure that we can support our scores well.

There are times when we may have missed something the employee has done and we need to adjust a score up. The employee brings data that we hadn't considered. It is your responsibility to make the final call on the score for an employee.

VPA-DS dispute resolution system

Employees must sign off on their VPA-DS stating that they agree with the assessment and that they were able to fairly present their views in the process. But there are times when both the boss and the employee can't agree on one or more items and the employee refuses to sign their assessment.

I've found that usually when this happens, someone (often the manager) didn't do their homework to substantiate their scores and now the employee isn't buying it. Also, a poor relationship between the two can also be the cause.

The manager is responsible to raise the issue with HR. The employee can initiate as well, but the manager is responsible to do so. HR will review the case and gather some facts from other sources if possible and will sit one-on-one with each to gain each person's perspective. These sessions can be very enlightening and may reveal that the disagreement has nothing to do with the performance issue but has its roots in something more personal.

HR then takes the situation to the manager's boss and together they decide on the final outcome. HR then discusses this outcome with the manager first and then with employee. You don't usually want to overrule your manager unless there's some hard evidence to demonstrate otherwise. A compromise in this situation is also a possibility.

The HR manager's job is to fully sell the decision to the employee ensuring that all of their issues have been heard and explored. The HR manager also provides the employee with further evidence to support the score. They can also tell the employee that their manager's boss has also reviewed their VPA-DS.

The final copy of the employee's VPA-DS is then signed by the employee, the manager, the manager's boss and HR. I stress this in order to get rid of poor managers. The boss's boss must get to know you to detect favoritism or root out a poor boss.

We developed this detailed process for resolution to demonstrate to our employees that we care about them and their development and that what they have to say is important. We also want to root out a bad manager and this process would help us identify such a situation. Also, if that employee ever comes up for dismissal down the road, you will be very familiar with them because of this history.

Tips for writing and conducting appraisals

Make sure you allocate enough time to conduct the appraisal without rushing. A VPA-DS would take me about four hours, plus or minus, for each employee just to write it. We spent up to two hours in the face-to-face appraisal. As expectations became more and more clear, the length of time decreased. Every employee wants their game time. Tell them why they did a good job and where they can improve.

Make sure you collect support on each employee throughout the year. Keep a file on each employee close at hand to write in and add any supporting material to. At the same time, remember to provide immediate feedback all along. Don't wait until the annual performance review to offer praise or spring a performance issue on the employee. Nothing frustrates the employee more than for them to think that everything is fine and then hit them with a negative review. That is extremely poor management and does not show your employees *respect*—a universal value.

I also scheduled quarterly review meetings with my employees as part of this process to ensure that they were receiving the feedback they needed. This also enabled us to discuss any issues on the progress of their performance with them. Most eagles take their reviews very seriously and can't stand not receiving top marks across the board. Once you provide very clear targets what they need to be top performers, they will work hard to achieve them. An eagle can't stand a poor review.

Lewis, a man I mentioned earlier, was my boss when I took the assignment to build the Contact Center in Cyprus. He was stationed in Toronto, CA, eight time zones removed. We had known each other for many years and he was a great boss. He had always seen me as an "A" and told me so.

When I went to Cyprus and set out to build the Contact Center from scratch, we had some huge hurdles to overcome. After a year we were making headway, but were still far from hitting our goals. Lewis conducted my performance review over the phone that year and ranked me as a "B".

I was truly devastated! I couldn't believe my ears. I had never been a "B" employee before. So I asked him to articulate for me what I needed to do to be an "A" in this position. One of the metrics he gave me was to become a world-class contact center.

I promised myself to never rank as a "B" employee again. In order to do this, I demanded clear expectations from my boss, so as to never fall into this trap again. I believe that many employees get fired, because expectations were never made clear to them.

In my experience, by about the third year, you'll find that you and the employee match your ratings almost all the time. And if you are off, it will only be by a little.

This process may seem like a lot of time and effort, but as we stated at the onset, people are your greatest resource and your true competitive advantage. This is why you need to spend this time on your employees and it will reward you well in the future. *This is the secret sauce, the cornerstone of this book.*

SUCCESSION PLANNING

The final phase of the performance development process is succession planning. Succession planning is the process by which you look at your whole team and determine who needs to improve and who needs to be promoted. Succession planning is much like drafting your team for the new football season.

Sticking with the football analogy for a moment, we start with the leadership of the organization. A pro-football team has their sights set on winning the Super Bowl. If they don't reach that goal, they re-evaluate what prevented them from reaching it.

The owners of that team review the whole lineup. Is the coach doing his job? Are there aging veterans or players past their prime who either need to retire or play for less money? Who on the team is a weak player and why are they weak? Who are your super stars and how can we maximize their talent?

Who are the strong, consistent players who show up and always play hard? Who will we recruit to fill the positions of the players that we cut? Where can we bring in a rookie and where do we need to recruit a high-dollar player with a proven record?

In a way very similar to a football team, we need to constantly improve our personnel each and every season.

We conducted the succession planning at year end, after the VPA-DS has been completed. Succession planning was a scheduled annual meeting in which we ranked all of the employees in the organization. We started with the lowest level managers ranking their employees and worked our way up through the organization to the top. You must rank your direct reports as well, just like every other manager and make the necessary changes.

In this way, we force-ranked every employee in the organization. This exercise not only reveals who your eagles, owls and seagulls are, but by ranking everyone, there are no ties between employees. This is absolutely necessary for a true succession plan.

Each manager would present his/her ranking to their next level manager. This process cascaded to the top until functional department heads presented their team to the senior management staff with supporting documentation.

We spent the most time on the "A's" in each department, ensuring that they were being fully utilized and had the "runway" they needed to continue to develop within the organization. As senior management, I believe it is mandatory that we get to know all the "A's" within the organization personally. These are our star players. We want them in the right positions and we want to train them, deploy them, and reward them appropriately.

Each manager would present their "A" employees individually and solicit feedback from the other senior managers to confirm or deny their ranking. If a manager disagreed with a ranking, they had to provide solid evidence to support their claim.

Once this process was completed, the team would force-rank the "A's" into one list. Having done that, we would start at the top and discuss future plans for each individual. This is how we facilitated cross-functional training. "A" employees could be recommended or chosen to move to another department or division in the company.

Obviously, not all "A's" will be the next CEO, but you should have two to five employees (depending on the size of the organization) that fit the criteria. These individuals should rise to the top of your ranking. Other "A" employees may have a ceiling of their competency at a senior level manager, so once they reach that level, they may become a "B" level employee.

The succession plan will show the final "goal" position for an employee and list the next one or two strategic promotions they need to fill for their development. When promoting someone we recognize three categories of promotion: the good fit; the stretch; and take a different job (lateral move to another department).

This practice emphasizes the importance of all senior level managers getting to know all the "A's" in the organization. When a senior manager receives an "A" employee in their department, they know who that employee is and why they are there.

The manager will not seek to undermine that employee, but support them to excel in their new assignment. In this way, we are constantly trying to develop the employee's skills, knowledge, and experience.

Once the team has thoroughly discussed all the "A" employees, we move down through the "B" employees and do the same thing. And finally we get to the "C" or "seagull" employees. We discuss them and what actions we are taking to turn them around. If we decide to let somebody go, we discuss this among the team so that everyone knows the situation and either agrees or disputes the decision.

When asked, Jack Welch said that his greatest regret in business was, "Not acting fast enough on poor performers." This was one of the greatest lessons I learned and helped us attain world class performance. Getting rid of dead wood will help you move forward, perhaps faster than anything else.

Sometimes a manager believes the "C" level employee is simply in the wrong job. In that case, we would seek to transfer them into a job more in line with their skills and talents.

The succession planning process is very involved, but do not allow your managers to become complacent. Guard against the mentality, "Hey, if you don't attack my employees, I won't attack yours." Good managers draw close to and are protective of their employees, which may color their thinking. This is one reason that we force-rank everyone in the organization. It requires us to provide objective support for ranking every employee.

I believe it was Brad Smart who observed that after a few years, a manager may find it more and more difficult to identify the "C's" in their department. He went on to say that every time a new manager is appointed to that department, without fail they found "C's".

Even after several years of values leadership, you will always have "C's" on your team. The reason for this is that not everyone can be the best when the whole team is forced-ranked. What this means is that you need to provide a plan that will help the "C's" to improve once again. The bar is continually rising. There will be a plan for the "C's", but they won't all be able to keep up with the organization and eventually you have to cut out the fat.

360-DEGREE REVIEWS

Every couple of years, we employed 360-degree reviews to gather more information about an employee. This type of review is especially helpful if the employee feels they are being unfairly or inaccurately ranked by you. The employee will see the results, but will not know who said what.

To conduct a 360-review appropriately, both the employer and employee choose two or three people from each of the following categories: the employee's subordinates, peers and superiors. Human Resources administers the evaluation and collates all the data providing a combined score.

Then the employee and the supervisor each receive a copy of the evaluation and meet to discuss the results. Typically, there will be disagreement around the values and how the employee sees themselves as opposed to how you and others observe them. But we let the results speak for themselves.

TRAINING AND DEVELOPMENT

The evaluation process is the most important performance-building tool in your organization. The training and development of your employees should be the follow up to that. You must spend 50 percent or more time on all of the people development processes and you (the leader) must own this process. As such, people development is a daily pursuit.

As with every other aspect of the employee's life with your organization, training and development must be inseparably linked with your values. Training and development are prerequisite for top performance, safety, quality, customer satisfaction, employee morale, low turnover, delegation, succession planning and nearly any other measure you can come up with.

Unfortunately, training and development (T&D) are usually relegated to the human resource department. In this way, T&D take a back seat. They are out-of-sight and out-of-mind as far as the leader is concerned. In this subordinated role, T&D are among the first to be cut when things get tight.

When T&D are not married to the values; and when T&D are not the primary responsibility of the leader, employees "go away for training." Then, when they return from training, they discover that their boss won't let them implement what they learned in the training. In fact, they may discover that the training runs counter to the values lived out on the factory floor.

This practice is so counter-productive and destructive to all that an organization wishes to accomplish! Paying mere lip service to training and development inflicts huge costs to the organization in terms of: expenses for training, time away from the job, damaged morale, unrealized gains, etc.

What we're advocating is the concept that the leader is responsible for the T&D of employees. Not that the leader does all the training, but the leader takes an active role in promoting it, ensuring its success, completion, and testing its results. This is a more integrated approach that combines all of the recruitment/ hiring, training/development, and performance management elements of an employee's life. The leader holds the employees accountable for their development and reviews their development in their performance evaluation.

A good training and development professional can prove their worth by helping create an integrated approach to all of those elements. In addition, the T&D professional can empower the leader and incumbent employees by engaging them in creating structured on-the-job training that is more effective and efficient than classroom models.

In the next chapter, we'll discuss how to achieve excellence through reporting and accountability.

Discussion Questions

1. Discuss the VPA-DS model. In what aspects of this model does your organization do well?

2. Using the VPA-DS model, in what ways can you improve the current processes in your organization?

3. In what ways does the VPA-DS model differ from what you are currently doing? What would you have to change in your organization in order to implement this tool?

4. Consider the level of priority you currently give training and development in your organization. How is training and development generally perceived in your company?

5. How might you leverage training and development to significantly improve performance?

CHAPTER NINE

Reporting and Accountability

Meetings get a bad rap, and deservedly so –
most are disorganized and distracted. But they can be a critical
tool for getting your team on the same page.
— Justin Rosenstein

Many have questioned the value of meetings and deem them a waste of time. I couldn't disagree more—as long as meetings serve a strategic purpose. A properly structured meeting that is on time and on task is one of the best ways to manage a team and keep everyone accountable. If people are saying that meetings are a waste of time in your organization then you are not running them correctly.

What does a bad meeting look like?

- Meetings start late and go over the allotted time
- Meeting participants go on and on and nobody stops them
- Side discussions are occurring
- Cell phones are going off and being answered (or texting)

- People get up in the middle of a meeting to take a call or do something else

- The purpose and goals of the meeting are unclear

- There's no follow up system in place to hold people accountable: no specific goals are set and the same problems keep cropping up

- There are no specific metrics presented at the meetings to track progress over time

- Everyone forgets what each member committed to at the previous meeting

On the contrary, well planned and executed meetings can provide us with a great context for reporting performance, solving problems, making decisions, communicating decisions, and building teamwork.

To set the tone for meetings, we decided we needed to start on time. This aligned with our value of respect for one another. For example, at the start people were coming late to meetings all the time. This phenomenon will grow if not kept in check. If one person arrives late with no repercussions, that gives others permission to do the same and so it goes. Before you know it, meetings are starting 15 to 30 minutes late, with the faithful sitting around waiting for everyone else. That is a huge time waster and shows disrespect for team members. Respect is so critical to this whole process.

To counter this problem we agreed to the rule that meetings must start on time, every time with no exceptions. We also instituted what we called the "Honey Pot" in the beginning. When someone was late for a meeting they had to put money in the Honey Pot. I can't remember why we called it that other than the fact that it was "sweet" for those who were on time because we later spent the money from the Honey Pot to buy treats, give to a charity, or go for drinks after hours.

The way the Honey Pot system worked was the first person late put in $5. A second late person had to double the amount to $10. A third late person doubled the amount again to deposit $20 in the Honey Pot and so on. This changes behavior quickly because you're measuring and managing it. Also, a system like this becomes more peer-managed than a heavy-handed boss approach. Once in place, the team supported and administered it.

What we discovered is that initially there was some grumbling and playful banter when someone came in late, but the "sting" of having to contribute to the Honey Pot kept them from a repeat performance. Then as the culture of the organization became more and more values-based, coming late to meetings disappeared altogether.

We left the Honey Pot on the meeting table even when it was no longer necessary. It served as a reminder of what once was and what our culture had become. That too was powerful.

SCHEDULING MEETINGS

In the matter of meetings we respected our people in other ways too. We always planned our meeting schedule a year in advance, putting all our regularly scheduled and special meetings on the calendar no later than December for the coming year. Then we sent the calendar to all impacted individuals and they booked their vacation schedules around the meeting schedule. They weren't allowed to plan their vacations during the quarterly off-sites, but they could miss weekly meetings. Once they had their vacations planned, we never infringed on their schedules. If we needed an emergency meeting, I'd work around *their* schedules instead of forcing mine on theirs.

The discipline of scheduling everything in advance not only showed respect for our employees, but also forced managers to plan and be very strategic and purposeful about our meetings. Scheduling all of our regular meetings like this also enabled us to require attendance for everyone invited to the meeting.

Our annual schedule of meetings included: annual review meetings, succession planning meetings, annual budget meetings, quarterly meetings (usually an offsite), weekly meetings, and any other mandatory meetings that the team was required to attend. The quarterly meetings were designed to tackle significant challenges like, "How are we going to tackle turnover?" The executive secretary maintained the planning schedule and updated it as needed.

ESTABLISH A HEALTHY MEETING CULTURE

Everyone in your meetings must feel that they have equal ground to share their ideas. For this reason, you must establish a culture for healthy debate. As the leader, be comfortable with not knowing all the answers. Your team is responsible for the solutions.

One way to create this safe, free-flowing culture is to refrain from sharing your ideas as a leader too early in the meeting. Listen to what others have to say and be open to changing your mind. If the boss blurts out what he/she is thinking first, this will stifle ideas from others. Who's going to challenge the boss? This is true especially in the early stages of the values-based organization. Later on, as the values permeate the organization, people will begin to challenge the boss in a healthy manner.

Your job is to ask lots of questions, not have all the answers. Be relentless with questions to ensure that everyone in the room, including you, is satisfied with the information. Explore dissenting views or other solutions with facts and debate. Try to push each solution to its max until it is either too logical to dismiss or its weaknesses are fully exposed.

Never steam-roll another person's solution or ignore it, for that will destroy the creative power of the team. Embrace the best practices of others including your competitors.

It takes time to develop this kind of trust. With some teams or groups you may find that it comes more quickly than with others, so be patient.

Also, create a culture in which everyone knows that all actions will be assigned, followed up on and reported. This sets a clear expectation and reinforces the effectiveness of a good meeting.

HOW TO RUN A WELL-TUNED MEETING

Even before you create an agenda, you must establish a structure for your meetings. This structure includes some specific roles: a chairperson, timekeeper, and an action-tracker.

Generally speaking, whoever calls the meeting is the chairperson. I serve as the chairperson for my meetings. The chairperson's role is to start and finish the meeting on time and to keep it on topic. If someone begins running off on a tangent or telling a story about how this relates to them, it's the chairperson's job to step in and redirect the conversation back on topic. The chairperson keeps the meeting on task. You must be relentless in this pursuit.

The time-keeper simply keeps track of time and lets the chairperson know how time is progressing. The time-keeper provides warnings five minutes, two minutes and one minute before the scheduled end of the meeting. The five-minute warning sends a message to everyone that we need to wrap things up and assists the chairperson in bringing closure. On the agenda, each topic was assigned a time limit.

If we ran out of time on a topic, I would ask whether this topic needed more time. If so, we voted to determine whether we would add time. With consensus we'd add time, but kept very tight tabs on it. This exercise in itself forced us to wrap up the discussion quickly.

The time-keeper role may sound extreme, superfluous, or even silly, but it accomplishes several things well. First, it separates monitoring time from the chairperson's role, making the chairperson accountable to the schedule. Second, if the time-keeper role is unassigned, everyone will become your time-keeper and you'll have a meeting full of clock-watchers. You want the meeting participants focused on the discussion, not the clock. Third, setting up a specific role for keeping time sends the clear message that time is important and we plan to respect the team members' time.

The time-keeper role can be assigned to anyone. In my meetings, I usually had my executive assistant keep time for us. But at other times the attendees would rotate into that responsibility.

The action-tracker role is also a very important one. The action-tracker is not a minutes-taker writing down everything that anyone said. That would be a complete waste of time and effort. Instead, the action-tracker only wrote down the actions steps agreed to in the meeting and who was assigned what by when.

For this role, we developed an *Action Tracker* form (*www. UnlockLeadershipCode.com*) that had the following headers over columns:

1. **Item number** – this is simply a sequential numbering of each issue.

2. The **topic or issue** with a brief description. A general topic may have multiple departments and people working on it, so we had a section for each functional group as well (e.g., finance, HR, etc.) Under each functional department, we recorded their world class metric target and their actual performance. For instance HR had a turnover rate goal of 5%, but perhaps actual was 90%. Having these goals ever before us ensured that we were pursuing what was truly important to us.

3. **Actions** – these are the clear and specific actions that we would take to address the issue.

4. **Outcomes** – for each action are clearly stated. The actions must be measurable and quantifiable so we knew what success looked like.

5. **Responsibility** – the names of those individuals responsible for the action and its outcome. We always tried to limit each action to a single person to bring more clarity and specificity to the action.

6. **Timing** – the day and month when this action would be completed. To the extent possible, we always tied an action to the calendar. Larger initiatives would have action steps tied to dates moving the whole toward completion. If the timing was later changed for any reason, we always kept the original date on the chart to show the delay.

All time commitments came from the employee responsible for carrying out the action. For this reason, I rarely had to police this. The team would challenge the employee if they provided an unrealistic target date. Because the employee gave the deadline, it increased their level of commitment.

7. **Status** – tracked the progress of the action toward its time-bound commitment. This column said either "on" or "off" track. If the action was "off-track", we also wrote a brief reason why. When an action was off-track, we color-coded it red, indicating a serious problem and a breach of commitment.

   Psychologically, the red box created tension in the meeting and the offending employee would do whatever it took to get it resolved. This is where you will see eagles soar and seagulls crap! An eagle rarely had a red box, but when they did, they handled the pressure gracefully and got it resolved quickly. Seagulls frequently have red boxes and even accumulate them. Seagulls breakdown under pressure.

   I know this sounds tough, but respect for your peers is extremely important. Delivering on what you promised and when you promised is critical for the team to succeed. If you can't deliver, then you're in the wrong job and it's time to move on. If an employee is missing targets and commitments, then they don't have a handle on their job. In this case, jump in, have a one-on-one and find out what's going on. Is this employee in over their heads?

8. **Miscellaneous** – captured things that might not be included in the action step, but would need to be discussed

at the next meeting. It could be an issue that we need to discuss that became apparent in the meeting, so we recorded it here to get it on the agenda for a future meeting.

MEETING AGENDA

Our meetings followed the same format every week, so the agenda itself didn't have to change too much from week to week. As I mentioned earlier, we scheduled our weekly meetings a year in advance.

We held our weekly meetings every Tuesday from 1-3pm. We chose Tuesdays because most long weekends fall on a Monday. This eliminated the need to reschedule around holidays and mess with people's schedules.

Also, we chose Tuesdays instead of Fridays because we wanted everyone focused on what they were going to do and accomplish that week. I wanted to ensure that they were focused on the right tasks for that week. Tuesday also allowed for the intensity and emotion of the meeting to carry through the entire week in order to get things done. Focus and priorities were set in this meeting. If someone had a red status box, that's all they thought about all week. A Friday, or end-of-the-week meeting loses the intensity and focus by the time Monday rolls around.

Tuesday meetings also meant that if a person had fallen behind on their commitments, they had the whole week and weekend to catch up if need be. The team did not readily accept the excuse, "I ran out of time."

The reason I scheduled the weekly Tuesday meetings at 1pm had to do with my personal time management system. I found that I was most productive between 6 and 11am, so I had that period blocked out and had my executive assistant gate-keep to protect that time. I had an open-door policy and would drop whatever I needed to if it was important during any other part of the day. But this morning block of time was mine to work on projects, strategy, presentations, etc.

You may have a different time that works best for you, but I suggest you find that time and protect it tenaciously. Your employees will understand and will adapt their schedules around yours. The only meeting I had in the morning was at 10am every day with my executive assistant (EA) for no more than 30 minutes. I had been working for four hours by then so I would have her project list completed. This gave her time to get organized before our afternoon meeting on Tuesdays.

She and I would work through the action items on the *Action Tracker* and prepare it for the afternoon meeting. In this way, the *Action Tracker* served as our agenda for each weekly meeting. We gave each issue 5-10 minutes, depending on the issue. Each department had a total of 15 minutes in the meeting. The last 30 minutes of the meeting we reserved for a special discussion.

After the weekly meeting, my EA would update the *Action Tracker* and send it out to the team no later than 10am the following day. The *Action Tracker* also provided a good source for supporting evidence for use with the VPA-DS process.

At the end of each month, we reviewed our performance against the 10 world-class metrics we had established. Each senior manager was responsible for one or more of these metrics. We recalibrated to the results and revised our action steps according to need.

OTHER KEY COMMUNICATION MEETINGS

Additional key meetings for improving communication included: town hall meetings, fireside chats and simply walking the floor.

We held **town hall meetings** frequently to communicate and present important information to the whole organization. We also used these meetings for question and answer sessions. In the town hall meetings we presented the employee satisfaction survey results.

Fireside chats were meetings that I set up with individual employees. My goal was to have at least one face-to-face meeting with every employee in the company per year. Employees usually had to be with the company for at least six months before we would schedule a fireside chat. If an employee managed others, I met with them more often: I met with my direct reports all the time, their direct reports two to four times a year. I knew all the managers well.

Before we met in a fireside chat, I asked employees to respond to three questions:

- What do you like most about working for us?
- What do you dislike most about working for us?
- If you could change anything, what would you change?

I also encouraged them to bring with them any other topic they'd like to discuss. The fireside chat broke the ice for many employees. They could see that I wasn't the big ogre in the corner office and that I actually had a personality. This opened the door for further communication later. They now felt comfortable walking up to me when I was walking the floor or saw me in the lunch room. I could also see who our eagles were. They had a lot to talk about and tried to impress me with prepared questions and solutions. These were my future stars.

The fireside chats were invaluable to me, helping me take the pulse of the organization and to ensure that senior management's message was getting through to the first-line employee. In my earlier days, when I managed the Western Canada Region, I made it a point to travel with the various sales reps on their territory. We had lots of time in the car to get to know each other driving sometimes for hours between calls...Canada is big!

These fireside chats helped me realize that no matter how clear I thought our message was, by the time it reached the front-line employee, it was often distorted, misinterpreted, or not heard at all. It's easy to think that you're communicating so well and that everyone is on board, but this quickly deteriorates as you move away through the organization. These fireside chats helped me calibrate with the employees. If I discovered too much missed information, we would develop a strategy for communicating that message better.

Walking the floor was something that I deliberately did daily and sometimes more than once. Often, if I needed to discuss something with someone, I left my office and sought them out. On my way, I would talk to people I met and at least acknowledge them with a smile. Your employees need to see you and feel comfortable talking with you.

The acknowledgement and smile are very powerful and set the tone for a values-based organization. It demonstrated confidence and control and employees want to work in that type of environment. They don't want to see a leader stressed and with his head down and get the sense that he thinks he is too important to talk to them.

I made it a point to know everyone's name. I would keep a list of all of our employees at my desk and make sure I knew the people on the list. In the early days when we had over 100% turnover this was a challenge.

There would be times when I would see someone in the hall or kitchen and I wouldn't know or remember their name. This would frustrate me, but I would go back to the office and pull out the list and then ask for help to identify who they were. I would also keep notes by each person's name to better remember them. I then made it a priority to talk to that employee in the next few days, so that I'd be better able to remember something about them.

Discussion Questions

1. On a scale of 1-10, 10 being outstanding and 1 being unacceptable, how would you rate the meetings in your organization?

2. How would others in your organization generally view meetings?

3. If you were to take the role of a consultant and seek to improve the meetings in your organization, what specific changes would you recommend in terms of scheduling meetings?

4. What changes would you recommend for establishing a healthy meeting culture?

5. What would you use meetings to accomplish in your organization?

6. What other meetings do you take advantage of in your organization? How might you leverage these for even greater impact?

7. To what extent do you get to know the employees in your organization? Why is this important? What are some things that you can do to excel at this?

8. How do you currently track and follow up meeting action steps? In what ways could you improve your process?

CHAPTER TEN
Core Values

When your values are clear to you,
making decisions becomes easier.
– Roy E. Disney

So far we've spoken a lot about values and the vital role they play in recruiting, hiring, training, leading, and managing performance. You've seen how crucial they are to your success as an organization. Core values are the set of guiding principles that your organization lives by. Your core values support your vision, shape the culture and reflect what the company deems important.

Values serve as the hub of the wheel that drives the performance of your organization and from which all decisions are made. Your core values inform the public, your customers, and all other constituents what your company is about, how you operate, and how you treat people. Core values function as your primary recruiting, evaluating and retention tools. Attention to your values will help you achieve peak performance.

Your core values serve as your code of conduct for operating on a daily basis. Your values shouldn't change with time, but are foundational to who you are. The organization controls its values entirely, unaffected by competitors, market conditions or other external factors.

The leaders in the organization must connect with and live out the values unequivocally. The success of the company depends on its leadership's adherence to the values. And only by alignment with the values by all employees can an organization achieve sustained maximum performance. If values become nothing more than words on a plaque, the organization will flounder. Values must become a living, breathing entity—front and center at all times—visible in every office, meeting room, work area and reception.

ESTABLISHING YOUR CORE VALUES

I have found that there is a universal set of core values that every corporation must follow. Integrity represents one such universal value, though an organization may use a different term to communicate it.

If you are a leader within an organization, you probably find yourself in one of a few different situations:

1. Perhaps you are part of a larger organization that already has established values. The organization may or may not communicate and live by their values, but you can adopt them and leverage them for the good of the organization. Even if your organization has a set of values, you may want to augment them with one or more to express the way your department or division will function.

2. Or it might be that you are part of a large organization, but to your knowledge they have never done the work it takes to develop a set of core values.

3. Maybe you are starting a company and have not yet established your core values.

Whichever your situation, I recommend that you go offsite for a retreat long enough that it allows you to conduct the vital work of developing and or integrating your core values. Plan to take your senior team with you on this offsite retreat and prepare them for this important work. Make sure that these are values you can't live without.

Also, develop a list of behaviors for each value. This is very important! You may want to hire a professional facilitator to help with this process and to keep the session on track and ensure that all members of the team participate in the development.

There's no magic number of values, but it seems to me that you want enough of them to express all that you desire to be, but keep the number few enough so people can readily remember them. I have found five or six values to be about right.

During your offsite, discuss how your values will impact the various aspects of running the business and integrate them into all those functions. Good values require tough decisions at times. If you establish values that are never challenged, your values may not be serving any real purpose. Watered down or generic values might be easy to uphold, but they also won't establish a strong culture. Companies with unique cultures tend to have values that are unconventional and sometimes controversial.

Below are some questions you can use to facilitate the values discussion:

- In what ways is this value important to our long-term success?

- To what extent can we say that we need to maintain this value forever?

- How sustainable is this value?

- To what degree does this value apply to all areas of the company and to all employees?

- In what ways will this value help us make important decisions in the future?

- If you woke up tomorrow morning with enough money to retire for the rest of your life, would you continue to hold on to this core value?

- Would you want the organization to continue to hold these values, even if at some point, they became a competitive disadvantage?

- If you were to start a new organization tomorrow in a different line of work, would you build these core values into the new organization regardless of its activities?

Strategies are sometimes confused with values because they answer the question how you are going to do something. The important difference is that strategies change as the competitive landscape changes, but values never change.

Some sample values might include:

- **Accountability** – Acknowledging and assuming responsibility for actions, products, decisions, and policies. This applies to both individual accountability on the part of employees and accountability of the company as a whole.

- **Balance** – Taking a proactive stand to create and maintain a healthy work-life balance for yourself and for your employees.

- **Commitment** – Committing to great products, services, and other initiatives that impact lives within and outside the organization.

- **Community** – Contributing to society and demonstrating corporate social responsibility.

- **Diversity** – Respecting and attending to the diversity of your community and organization. Establishing an employee equity program.

- **Empowerment** – Encouraging employees to take initiative and give their best. Adopting a failure-embracing environment to empower employees to lead and make decisions.

- **Innovation** – Pursuing new creative ideas that have the potential to change the world.

- **Integrity** – Acting with honesty and honor without compromising the truth.

- **Ownership** – Taking care of the company and customers as if they were one's own.

- **Safety** – Ensuring the health and safety of employees and going beyond the legal requirements to provide an incident-free workplace.

In that offsite meeting, you'll want to discuss how to roll out the values for your employees. The roll-out and communication of your values depends on too many factors to discuss here. But make sure to devise a communication and implementation plan consistent with your values! It's important to communicate to your employees that while some things will no doubt change over the years, the values will not. Give them permission to hold you and each other accountable to the values.

OUR VALUES CREATION PROCESS

As I suggested, we took a three-day off-site with the senior team to develop our own specific set of core values. To prepare for the meeting, I showed my team examples of values from other corporations. I also had them read some articles and books on values.

None of this team had ever participated in an off-site like this before and some of them were in a panic when I told them they'd be out of the office for three whole days! Getting away on a small island was a challenge because for most of us, home was no more than an hour away. The team struggled with this at first and couldn't understand why they couldn't go home at night.

But by the end of our three days, they realized the importance of that three-day getaway. It changed us profoundly as a team and how we worked together in the future. Getting away from work and other distractions was vital to focusing on the work at hand and for building our team. We did schedule breaks so the team could respond to calls and emails.

The first day, we spent all day discussing what values are, why they're important and how they can transform an organization.

The next day, we posted everything around the room that we wanted to cover and discussed what values were important to us and why.

On the final day, we took everything we had discussed and distilled the values to a short list. We also included specific actions for each value. Attaching actions to the values is crucial because they give you the means for evaluating employee performance.

Depending on the size of the team and level of engagement, the offsite could be longer or shorter. But I doubt you could accomplish a meaningful and lasting values creation and implementation plan in one day. After our third day, we walked away with a rough draft of our core values and their associated actions. We followed up with dedicated meetings back at the office to fine-tune and polish this list.

The six core values we came up with are as follows:[7]

⚜ Do the right thing with integrity by

- Being honest with ourselves and respecting others
- Being transparent, saying what we mean and meaning what we say

⚜ Perform by

- Having the passion to be the best, setting stretch targets and rewarding results
- Taking ownership and being accountable for your actions and results
- Being fact based, objective and accurate
- Having the self-confidence to operate responsibly without boundaries

※ Take Action by

- Being proactive

- Encouraging the freedom to challenge or disagree

- Taking measured risks without a fear of failure

- Having the sense of urgency in everything we do

- Eliminating bureaucracy

※ Continuously Improve by

- Constantly learning, teaching and sharing

- Embracing change as an opportunity not a threat

- Living quality, reducing costs for competitive advantage

※ Think Outside the Box by

- Being customer-centric

- Thinking globally and boundary-less, ideas can come from anywhere in any industry

※ Have Fun by

- Choosing our attitude

- Making someone's day

- Being present, participative and actively engaged always

Our values required that we create a culture of risk taking and learning from mistakes. Mistakes must be a welcome forum for learning. Break the school-based notion that mistakes are wrong and abandon the "red ink" syndrome associated with them.

The behaviors associated with each value helped us quantify and measure the values in the evaluation process (VPA-DS process).

COMMUNICATING AND LAUNCHING THE VALUES

Once we completed the selection of values, we communicated them to all the employees via a question and answer period. We wanted to make sure we could clearly articulate them and that they were understood.

Rolling out the values like this was only the first step, so don't expect any miracles yet! The employees may say they understand them, but they really don't at this point. In fact, not even the management team understands how to apply them or the full extent of how the values will influence and impact the organization.

The next step we took was to break up the employees into six cross-functional teams and assign each team one value. The teams were cross-functional so they were engaged in this exercise with people they did not normally work with.

In this exercise, we told the employees we were going to host a "Carnival of Values" and each team was to design a booth at the carnival that would clearly demonstrate that particular value. We gave each team a small budget for materials. The booths had to be "live" with some kind of active participation going on at each booth in order to engage the employees. Each booth was to hand out a small values-related prize.

We asked the teams to organize themselves and manage their work on their booths primarily on their own time. This helped instill teamwork and working together for the greater cause of the organization. The teams were given a room somewhere in the building in which to build their booth and a deadline for completing it. The teams were sworn to secrecy and satellite development areas were created to keep the teams' work from view.

Of course there were challenges with this whole undertaking as we were a 24/7 operation. Also, some people took more leadership, or did more work than others, but that's to be expected. There will always be teams who dive deep into the process and others who don't.

Having several teams and putting them in separate rooms, giving them a month to prepare increased the competition. The employees would talk in the halls and find out what the other teams were doing. This motivated the weaker teams to take on more responsibility and run pace with the stronger teams. This form of competition was beautiful!

During the carnival, all booths were to be staffed by members of that team on a rotating basis. Additionally, we asked all employees to visit each of the other booths. While at a booth, an employee experienced some sort of activity to impress on them the meaning of that value. Then, each employee had to be signed off by that team indicating that they understood this value and had completed all that value's activities. Then they received the prize for that value.

The company provided all the food and refreshments for the carnival. We took pictures of all the booths, the fun and activities and made albums, distributing them to everyone. Overall, the values carnival was a tremendous success and set the proper tone for building our culture around our six values.

We left the booths up for a week as a reminder of the importance of the values and the new company culture that they represented.

Following the values carnival, we intentionally talked about our values with our employees at every opportunity and in every venue imaginable. These included: our pizza Fridays, coffee with management, themed parties, the break room, kitchen, and town hall meetings. Additionally, we introduced our customers, partners, and other constituents to our values.

Our value: *have fun* was new to me at the time, but we all felt this was an important value. This was especially relevant because the majority of our employees were on the front lines bearing the brunt of customer complaints. We wanted a way to ensure focus on fun as a way to relieve the stresses of the job.

In order to make good on having fun, we created a dedicated lounge area for games, a TV with a large assortment of DVDs, etc. Our operation was 24/7 and employees needed a place to relax at night in particular, but also on breaks and lunches. We threw month-end Friday pizza parties, which provided senior management additional opportunities to get to know and talk with employees from all departments. We also planned quarterly themed parties to celebrate a specific accomplishment.

IMPLEMENTING THE VALUES

Once the values have been established and communicated, the CEO and the senior staff are responsible to keep the values at the top of the minds of every employee at all times. Earlier in my career, when I was first introduced to a core set of values that the company had developed, these were consistently involved in everything we did.

When introducing the values for the first time, it may seem a little odd to the organization. But with senior management never letting them disappear, they begin to seep into the deepest cracks of the organization. The values really begin to take hold when the employees experience their first performance evaluation and recognize that the values constitute 50% of their evaluation. This is especially true if bonuses or promotions are tied to values performance.

At first, your employees will think that they understand the values, what they mean and how they're applied. After all, many of the values may mirror personal values (though never expressed) of your employees already. But as you begin to evaluate employees on the basis of whether they are conducting themselves by the values, they begin to realize that there is much more to this than meets the eye.

For instance, in a performance review if you ask an employee to give you an example of how they have demonstrated or exhibited a particular value, they begin to grasp the fuller meaning and application of these values. After the first set of evaluations you can start to see things change in the organization. The first evaluation is really an orientation and values-alignment session.

The easier values are the first to be demonstrated. For example, one of our values was "Dare to be transparent." This value meant, for instance, that all employees were empowered to eliminate all politics and status in a meeting. Facts trumped everything and it was the employee's responsibility to communicate those facts no matter how difficult or embarrassing they may be. By doing this, the organization recognized transparency as a core value, so there could be no repercussions for stating facts—even if you were challenging the CEO. There was no hierarchy in these meetings and no repercussions for challenging anyone.

If things began heating up in a meeting, leaders or other employees in the organization would raise their hand and say, "I dare to be transparent..." and then they would speak the facts. At first this sounded odd, but everyone knew what it meant and no one could attack that person or hold any grudges for stating the facts. This proved very effective in our meetings and elsewhere.

As employees witness this and other examples of the values in their everyday encounters, the application of the values spreads into all aspects of work and throughout the organization. Employees move from being values-aware to values-believing, values-practicing and values-consistent.

In the VPA-DS, we scored each value on a scale of Role Model, Potential Leader, Progressing, and Needs Improvement. In the first round of evaluations after introducing the values, this produced scores between Needs Improvement and Progressing on average for the organization. As the organization became more comfortable with the values and actually started practicing them the scores moved into the Potential Leader—Role Model range. Role Model scores were given out to the true leaders of that value.

As a manager evaluating employees on values, I would always find one person who exemplified a particular value. That person stood out as a role model for that value. This was a person for whom there was no dispute that they were *the leader* in demonstrating that value. I would use them as the Role Model and everyone else would be rated against the leader for that value.

I would discuss this openly with the employee in the evaluation process. It is critical for employees to see who the standard is in that value so they can calibrate to that standard. Then you need to provide them with concrete examples of how that value is lived and practiced in the organization.

If there was no role model for a particular value, then we came up with the "gold standard" for that value and provided the employee with specific examples of that value within the scope of their job. And of course, the actions associated with each value helped tremendously in casting that "gold standard."

Discussion Questions

1. Discuss why leaders within an organization must unequivocally adhere to their company's values.

2. What is the status of your organization right now in terms of owning, articulating and operating by a clear set of values?

3. What are your organization's core values?

4. In what ways do you think your organization needs to grow with respect to its core values?

5. How do you currently communicate and reinforce your core values? In what ways can you improve this?

6. What one thing are you taking away from this chapter that you will implement within the next 30 days?

CHAPTER ELEVEN

Vision and Mission

Vision is everything for a leader. It is utterly indispensable.
Why? Because vision leads the leader.
– John C. Maxwell

VISION STATEMENT

In contrast to the mission or purpose statement, a company's vision statement describes *who we strive to become.* The vision statement is usually an inspirational description of what an organization would like to achieve or accomplish. The vision serves as a lofty pursuit that directs our current and future actions.

With uncanny clarity, Helen Keller said, "The only thing worse than being blind is having sight but no vision." And George Washington Carver said, "Where there is no vision, there is no hope." We owe it to our organization and to our employees to lead with crystal clear vision.

PK. Bernard warns, "A man without a vision is a man without a future. A man without a future will always return to his past."

People who insist on living in the "good ol' days" can't envision beyond what has been. Finally, Kris Vallotton said, "If your memories are greater than your dreams, then you're already dying."

The vision statement may answer questions like:

- Where would we like to be as an organization in 5 years?
- What can we be best at in the world?
- What do we want to be passionate about?
- What do we want to become?

As the word "vision" implies, it must present a clear picture of our business goals or targets. Again, the mission describes what we're about; the vision shows the ultimate results of our end-state, or final result. The vision is what we aspire to be. Vision keeps us all focused on the same goal.

For the leader, vision becomes the rallying point for all employees. Vision helps us to see by faith what may not even be possible at this moment. That was certainly true of President John F. Kennedy's visionary speech at Rice University on September 12, 1962, in which he challenged America to put a man on the moon. We didn't even possess the technology required to put men on the moon, but JFK's vision for it got us there.

Likewise, FedX created a vision for delivering mail and packages overnight—something that was unheard of before, but they have now taught us to expect. FedX wanted to become number one. They decided that overnight delivery would get them there. They envisioned their future state and created a gap analysis to determine how to become what they envisioned.

Other examples of vision statements include:

- **Amazon:** "Our vision is to be earth's most customer centric company; to build a place where people can come to find and discover anything they might want to buy online."

- **Nike:** "To bring inspiration and innovation to every athlete in the world."

- **Oxfam:** "A just world without poverty."

- **Avon:** "To be the company that best understands and satisfies the product, service, and self-fulfillment needs of women—globally."

- **Starbucks:** "To share great coffee with our friends and help make the world a little better."

- **Hilton:** "To fill the earth with the light and warmth of hospitality."

In developing your vision statement, you may want to explore issues such as:

- What will keep us focused and committed to in the same direction?

- Where will our industry be in five years?

- What will competition in our industry be like in five years?

- What is our sustainable competitive advantage?

- What technology do we not possess that we'll need in five years?

- What can we do that no one else can?

- In what ways do our customers benefit from our products and services?

%% What difference do we want to make in the world?

%% What lofty stretch-goal will propel us into the future? The "Manhattan Project"— it's world-changing.

%% Where would you like to be, compared with where you are today (by some specific measure)?

If you need to develop a vision or mission statement, I recommend doing so at an offsite retreat with your senior staff. As with values development, you may wish to engage the help of a professional facilitator to direct the process and keep you on course.

In application, the vision serves the leader to help him/her move their people from "here" to "there" (that future state). Armed with the vision, the leader must first clearly communicate that staying "here" is out of the question. The leader must convince the organization that remaining in its current state is undesirable, untenable, and unthinkable.

Next, the leader must cast vision for what could be and generate excitement and buy-in for pursuing that vision.[8] From then on out, the drive is to realize what has been envisioned for the organization. Nothing else is acceptable.

Leadership guru Bill Hybels also cautions, "Everyone's vision bucket leaks. So the leader must continually refill it by taking people back to the vision."[9] In a manner similar to what we described regarding values, we must constantly and consistently speak about the vision: where we're headed and why we're headed there. We keep reminding the organization what's at stake and how great the rewards will be once we attain our vision.

MISSION STATEMENT

Although this book revolves around an organization's core values, vision and mission are also fundamental tools that an organization and its leaders cannot do without. A mission statement articulates *why* we exist. It broadcasts to employees and the world: "This is our mission, our purpose."

An organization's mission statement is a formal declaration of their core purpose or focus. In a nutshell, a company's mission states why it exists. The mission is the big idea statement. It answers the question, "We do what?" The mission declares what services and/or products the organization strives to offer.

The mission spells out the underlying motivation for being in business in the first place. It describes the contribution the firm aspires to make for society. I believe the best mission statements are short, sharp and clear. Walt Disney's mission statement: "We make people happy," clearly demonstrates that.

The mission statement also forces focus. The company cannot be all things to all people. Many companies lose their way with an ambiguous or unstated purpose.

Some examples of mission statements are listed below:

- **New York Times:** "The core purpose of The New York Times is to enhance society by creating, collecting and distributing high-quality news and information."

- **General Electric:** "We have a relentless drive to invent things that matter: innovations that build, power, move and help cure the world. We make things that very few in the world can, but that everyone needs. This is a source of pride. To our employees and customers, it defines GE."

❦ **Sony:** "At Sony, our mission is to be a company that inspires and fulfills your curiosity. Our unlimited passion for technology, content and services, and relentless pursuit of innovation, drives us to deliver ground-breaking new excitement and entertainment in ways that only Sony can. Creating unique new cultures and experiences. Everything we do, is to move you emotionally.

❦ **Wal-Mart:** "We save people money so they can live better."

❦ **Coca-Cola Corporation:** "To refresh the world...to inspire moments of optimism and happiness...to create value and make a difference."

❦ **Starbucks:** "Our mission: to inspire and nurture the human spirit one person, one cup and one neighborhood at a time."

❦ **Barton Publishing:** "We empower people to experience vibrant and amazing health through natural healing remedies."

Some questions you can pose to evaluate or create a mission statement may include:

❦ How understandable is your mission statement?

❦ How actionable is it?

❦ How specific and descriptive is it?

❦ To what extent does your mission statement:

  ▪ Excite people?

  ▪ Motivate people to stretch?

❦ Balance the possible with the impossible?

- Give people a clear sense of the direction and profit-ability of the company?

- Inspire people to feel they are part of something big and important?

※ There are many great books out there to help you develop a mission statement, but this book is not designed to help you do that.

VISION, MISSION, VALUES AND STRATEGY

Our vision, mission, values and strategies all work together to enable us to move forward in concert. Our vision sets a lofty goal before us, reminding us who we wish to become. Our mission reminds us what we're about. Our vision inspires passion and zeal, while mission promotes creativity, perseverance and sacrifice.

Our goals/targets, strategies, and tactics provide us with a daily game-plan for fulfilling our mission and reaching our vision.

Finally, our values define our moral, ethical and social bearing. The values are our character. They govern the way in which we carry out our vision, mission, and strategies. Values are also the backbone of our performance management system.

But what so many organizations fail to see is that *values are the road to financial success.* When values are leveraged to improve performance, they become powerful engines for increasing an organization's profits.

Referring back to the VPA-DS performance review process, remember 50% of an employee's performance is measured in terms of adherence to the values; and performance to objectives addresses the rest: the pursuit of vision, mission, strategies and goals.

Discussion Questions

1. What is your organization's vision statement? In what ways does it influence your performance goals?

2. In what ways could you exploit your vision statement to inspire creativity, perseverance and sacrifice?

3. What is your company's mission statement? To what extent does it drive your performance goals?

4. In what ways could you leverage your mission statement to motivate employees and fulfill your purpose as an organization?

5. As a result of reading this chapter, what will you do differently, or put into action?

CHAPTER TWELVE

Conclusion

We will not become number one with better sameness.
– AJ Slivinski

The Leadership Code builds the foundation of your organization through people, who are your most valuable and strategic asset. The Leadership Code customizes to you and your business, because it incorporates *your* values as the cornerstone of your business.

The quality of the people you lead will take you where you want to go as long as you provide them with the environment in which they can flourish. If you neglect your people, as so many managers do, your fate is already sealed. If, on the other hand, you invest in them, spend time with them, challenge them, hold them accountable, train them, and reward them they will exceed all expectations.

Remember we used the analogy of bread-making at the beginning of this book. We talked about the fact that making delicious bread is not just about having the right ingredients. Any organization can go through the motions of gathering all the right ingredients: values, mission, vision, strategy, performance review process, and even hiring great people.

But it's *the people-focused, values-based leader* who can skillfully blend them all together to achieve absolutely amazing results. Many managers today only think in terms of numbers and bottom line performance. They are not leaders who empower and inspire their employees to accomplish remarkable performance.

We said earlier that values are like the hub of a bicycle wheel, with its many spokes representing the employees. A manager who disregards the values and employees is essentially trying to pedal a bike without wheels. He or she may be pedaling for all their worth, but they're not going anywhere.

World-class leadership requires doing the simple things right and not over-complicating things. It's the combination of every one of these things: great leadership, treating people with respect, leading meetings well, values-based performance reviews, etc., that lead to consistent, ever-increasing success. The genius is in doing every single one of these things in concert, unswervingly, without fail.

This book bears the title The Leadership Code. Think in terms of writing *code* for a computer program. The lines of code need to be precise and consistent. Change one character in a line of code and the program either won't run, or it will do something other than desired. The Leadership Code contains all the elements required to launch and grow a successful business.

We are convinced that as you apply the principles of The Leadership Code in your organization, you will experience the same kinds of improvements, performance and financial success that we have.

We believe that The Leadership Code offers any organization a winning competitive advantage. None of the principles we shared in this book are new. But they are basic to leading and managing an organization well. The reason that following these basic principles provides an organization with a significant competitive advantage is that so few leaders are willing to discipline themselves and their organizations to live by them. It's as simple as that.

We've provided the recipe—The Leadership Code for achieving world-class performance—the rest is up to you. If this book has merely whetted your appetite for more, please visit our website: *www.UnlockLeadershipCode.com.*

An organization's ability to learn,
and translate that learning into action rapidly,
is the ultimate competitive advantage.
– Jack Welch

FREE RESOURCES FOR READERS OF
THE LEADERSHIP CODE

As a reader of this book, you are entitled to free Members Only Access to our Leadership Code Resource Library. This library is filled with valuable resources, and we will add to it periodically. Inside the Members Area you will discover the following forms, checklists and tools:

Values
- Sample Values
- Questions Developing Your Values
- Our 6 Values and Behaviors

Leadership and Communication
- 2 Leadership Lessons
- Direct vs. Consensus Leadership
- 9 Traits of a Good Mentor
- 4 Keys to Ensure Positive Relationship
- 4 Fireside Chat Questions
- 9 Post Hiring Questions
- 10 Ways to Frustrate Your Employees
- 6 Ways to Derail Team Development
- 9 Clues for a Bad Meeting

Planning
- Strategic Waterfall (PDF)

Performance Management
- VPADS Evaluation Form (PDF)
- 7 Critical Elements of Performance Evaluation
- Values Performance Matrix
- Action Tracker (PDF)
- Our 10 World Class KPI's
- Sample Chart of Employee Performance Measurement

Employee Behavior
- Defining the Birds of Performance
- ABC Employees Defined
- 30 Key Hiring Traits
- 4 Assessment Areas for Employees
- 8 Reasons Employees Stay
- 10 Reasons Employees Leave

To claim your free Members Only Access to our Leadership Code Resource Library, visit:
UnlockLeadershipCode.com/members

Endnotes

1 Statistic Brain, "Startup Business Failure Rate by Industry," January, 1, 2014, *http://www.statisticbrain.com/startup-failure-by-industry/*.

2 Bloomberg Business Week, "The Living Company: Habits for Survival in a Turbulent Business Environment," nd, *http://www.businessweek.com/chapter/degeus.htm*.

3 Andrew Gordon, "Why America's Most Powerful Companies Are Dying Off," Early Investing, February 14, 2014, *http://earlyinvesting.com/americas-powerful-companies-dying-off/*.

4 Carmen Nobel, "Why Companies Fail—and How Their Founders Can Bounce Back," Harvard Business School, March 7, 2011, *http://hbswk.hbs.edu/item/6591.html*.

5 1 Corinthians 15:33, Holy Bible, New International Version®, NIV® Copyright © 1973, 1978, 1984, 2011 by Biblica, Inc.® Used by permission. All rights reserved worldwide.

6 Brad D. Smart, PhD, *Top Grading* (New York: Portfolio/Penguin, 2012).

7 I am greatly indebted to Maple Leaf Foods, where I learned the importance of core values and how they should drive all that we do as an organization. Maple Leaf's values provided a great foundation for us as we developed our own similar core values at the Contact Center.

8 Bill Hybels, "Leaders Move People from Here to There," The Global Leadership Summit, August 5, 2010.

9 Bill Hybels.

Made in the USA
Middletown, DE
28 April 2017